Old Blackburn and Darwen

by Albert Forrest

To my grandsons

John and David Forrest

Cover illustrations:

Front: *A view of King William Street in 1906, showing the market, dominated by its famous and much-loved (and much-lamented) clock tower. This building was one of the greatest losses that Blackburn has sustained in architectural terms since 1945.*

Background: *A small section of the huge crowd that watched the dedication of the War Memorial and Garden of Remembrance in Preston New Road on 2 August, 1924.*

Contents

Old Blackburn and Darwen
by Albert Forrest

Copyright, © Albert Forrest, 1990

First edition, July 1990

Typeset in Times and Caslon Medium by Carnegie Publishing Ltd.
Published by Carnegie Publishing Ltd., 18 Maynard Street, Preston PR2 2AL
Printed by Mather Brothers Printers Ltd. (a member of the Pindar Group), Preston.

ISBN 0 948789 56 5

Old Blackburn and Darwen

Work

HE life of the town and its people centred around work: the hardness and harshness of it, the inevitability of it, the poor pay at the end of it, the dirt and danger and drudgery of it, the terrible hardship to be faced without it. My mother, born in 1864, went to work in a cotton mill at eight years of age. Her schooling had been negligible: she could neither read nor write. In her time even boys and girls as young as six or eight still worked in the mines and the factories. They were regarded as expendable, there was not the wherewithal to keep them, and they were not wanted. The death rate for infants in Manchester and Liverpool was around sixty per cent, and in Blackburn and Darwen it was not much better.

Blackburn and Darwen were cotton towns. In earlier times, handloom weaving had been a very important part of the towns' economies. The distinctive long windows of handloom weavers' cottages, which provided enough light for the work of the weavers to continue late into the summer evenings, were common features all around the area. Some of them can still be seen today, as around Revidge and elsewhere. Even as early as the 1700s, there were large numbers of people weaving cotton in their own homes, many of them using this as a significant extra source of income to supplement what they could glean from smallholdings or other trades. Such were the profits to be made from handloom weaving in the early years that whole familes turned to cotton as the mainstay of their existence.

The weaving of checked cloths and calicos on the handloom were thus very important cottage industries for the inhabitants of Blackburn Darwen, Mellor and Tockholes, and many isolated cottages and farmhouses. Enterprising gentry had provided the weavers with the raw materials and later had collected the woven pieces which were then stored in warehouses, and made ready for marketing, distributed by the aid, very often, of packhorses.

With the development of the fly-shuttle by John Kay in 1733, the spinning jenny by Richard Arkwright and Samuel Crompton in 1769 and 1779 respectively, the cottage industry had become a disaster. The inventions were received by its workpeople with savage hostility. Although it took some time for such inventions to be widely adopted, when they became more common it obviously had the effect of reducing costs considerably; this led to a marked fall in wages for the handloom weavers, whose livelihoods became more and more precarious. Weavers were forced to work longer and longer hours for less and less pay. Naturally, they blamed the new inventions, and they sought their revenge in the destruction of machinery and in the burning of mills.

On Monday 24 April 1826, a mob of angry weavers from Blackburn, Whalley, Clitheroe, Haslingden and Accrington set out to wreak destruction on weaving sheds with home-made pikes and staves, and some with sledge-hammers. They broke up power-loom machinery at Accrington, Rossendale, Darwen and Salford Hundred; and at Chorley a mob of about six thousand marched in the direction of Blackburn. That same evening thousands of excited weavers paraded in the streets boasting that not a single power-loom in the neighbourhood had been left unbroken.

Nevertheless, Lancashire was ideally suited for the development of the cotton industry. The mountain streams could provide water power for the early spinning machinery and, later, when steam took the place of water, the climate provided the warmth and moisture needed for several of the processes. There were many reasons for the huge expansion of the cotton industry on the west of the Pennines, not least the availability of cheap, experienced labour, and of capital to fund the new mills. In many towns, factory blocks began to appear. Rows of houses (or should I say hovels) were being built to shelter the swarms of people needed by the new factory system.

The whole cotton structure was also bedevilled by economic recessions, short-time working and cyclical growth. The worst such period came at the time of the American Civil War, when the terrible cotton famine of 1861-3 brought a renewed period of hardship and

Rioters in Darwen Town Centre — a woodcut from the Illustrated London News.

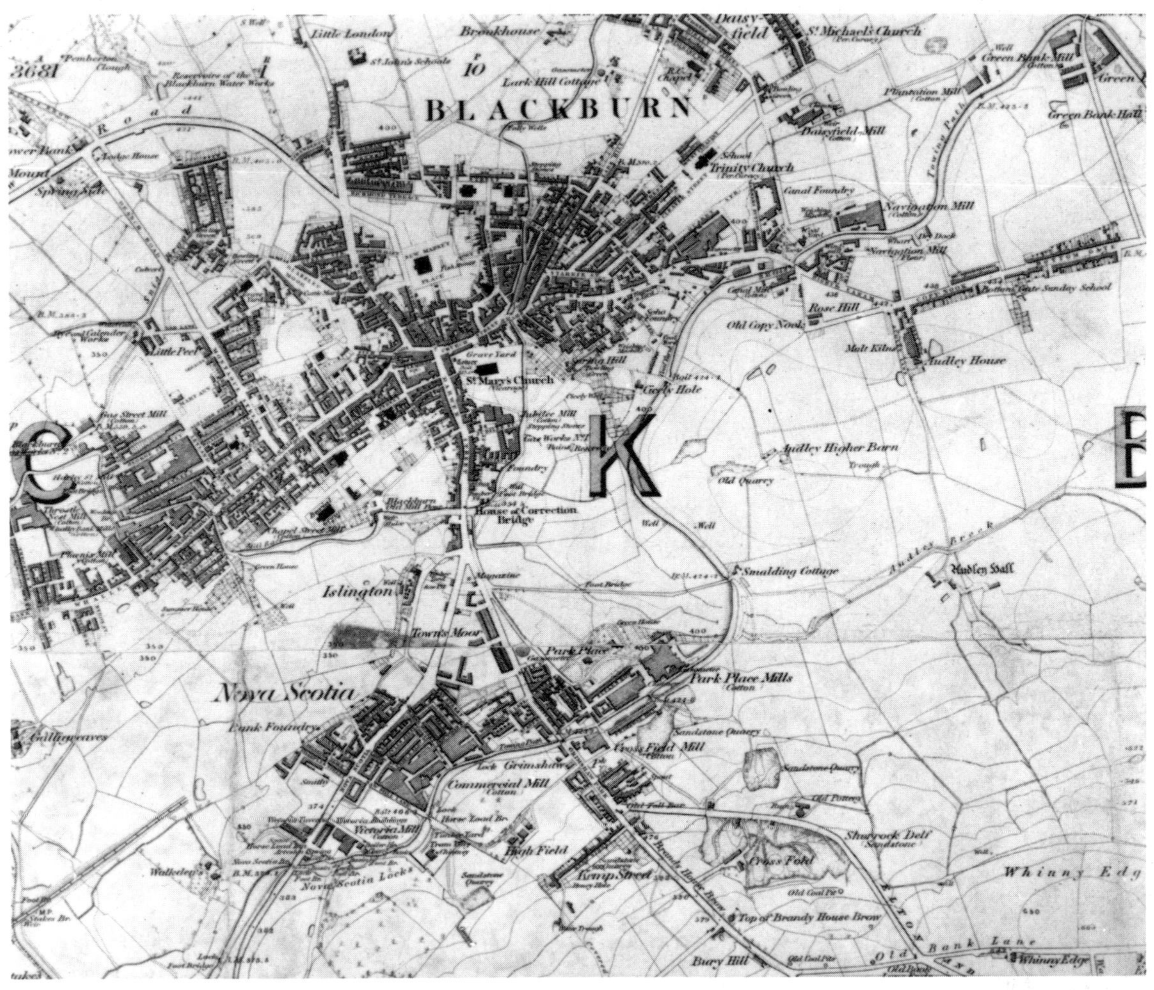

Blackburn in 1848. This map is the first-edition Ordnance Survey map and shows the new industrial areas which had developed around Nova Scotia and Eanam. The Leeds and Liverpool Canal was very important in influencing the location of the new factories – the vast majority of which were built along or near to its banks.

suffering, since some 85% of the raw cotton came from America. Towards the end of 1862, 32,000 people in Blackburn alone had become dependent on charity. By Christmas more than half a million in Lancashire towns were receiving regular free meals. Efforts were made to find alternative work; in Blackburn, for example, hundreds of mill workers were working on improvements within the new Corporation Park which had been opened in 1857.

By the time that my mother was born, therefore, powerloom and factory working had become firmly established in Blackburn and Darwen. From the time the needy people were born they were destined to work in the mills, without much hope of choosing a career. Their minds were blunted; they had almost no education and few were literate. They were wakened, year in and year out, by the five o'clock blower or by the knocker-up with his long stick, rattling on the bedroom window. There would be no fire in the grate and no hot water for a drink or a wash (in one mill the management recommended that all their workpeople should wash themselves at least twice a week).

Mothers would get their children up at four-thirty in the morning, bundle them in a basinette, and take them to grandma or to a child-minder's cottage. At dinner time the older children would take the babies to the mill to be breast-fed by their mothers. The mother's meal would probably be bread and dripping, packed up the night before in a red handkerchief.

Hurrying to the mill the mother would join the hundreds of other ghostly shapes in their grey shawls, clattering over the cobblestones in their clogs: the noise and the clatter would be deafening. To be five minutes late at the mill would mean a fine of sixpence, and that out of a wage of eight shillings a week would be a very serious matter: the difference between eating and not eating. If the gate keeper was in a bad mood, in keeping with the weather, he might have closed the gate and she would have to go back home.

If the family became destitute, because the breadwinner was out of work, the Overseers of the Poor would send some or all of them to the workhouse. The children would be separated from their parents, and all would be in misery, distress and humiliation.

By the time I was at school it was a little better, but not a lot. The employment of children in the mills and mines had ended, and I stayed at school until I was thirteen years old. I wanted to be a draughtsman in a drawing office, but eventually was pushed into an engineering works at 1½d. an hour (3½p). Eventually I finished my time there as a toolmaker, which was a highly skilled trade.

The first step towards 'social security' came when Lloyd George introduced the government scheme in 1906 and the years following. For the first time in history schoolchildren were given one good square meal a day. Medical inspections were held in the schools, to nip ailments and diseases in the bud. By sticking a fourpenny stamp each week on your National Insurance card you could receive free medical treatment and sick pay for several weeks. The state pension for old people protected them from the threat and fear of spending their declining years in gruelling hard work, loneliness and humiliation in the dreaded workhouse.

The Blakewater, once a clear country stream rising in the bowl of hills encircling Blackburn, was used as a source of water power from early times. In the eighteenth century the development of industry using the river for power meant that its banks became lined with mills and factories, while the waters themselves were constrained by high stone walls. In this view, taken about 1920, there are several early mills, including a corn mill nearest to the camera. Its age is indicated by its being built of rough and irregular stone slabs, the traditional material of the pre-industrial age. The Blakewater itself, a dirty polluted trickle, runs almost unnoticed in its deep artificial channel. Large parts of the stream had already been culverted by this date, a process which has continued to the present day. The result is that long stretches in the centre of Blackburn are now invisible, nothing more than a buried pipeline.

As the Industrial Revolution proceeded, the Leeds and Liverpool Canal (opened in 1816) provided a new focus for the building of mills, offering, as it did, cheap and easy transport of essential coal supplies and other raw materials, and of the finished cloth. Eanam and Higher Eanam were photographed from the air about 1930, and the confusion of mills, with their tall chimneys, long rows of closely-packed terraced housing, churches, warehouses and narrow roads, is clear. The area had grown up piecemeal, without planning. More recently, 'progress' has swept away much of this scene, although the Eanam canal wharves are undergoing restoration as an amenity and heritage site as part of the Leeds and Liverpool Canal project.

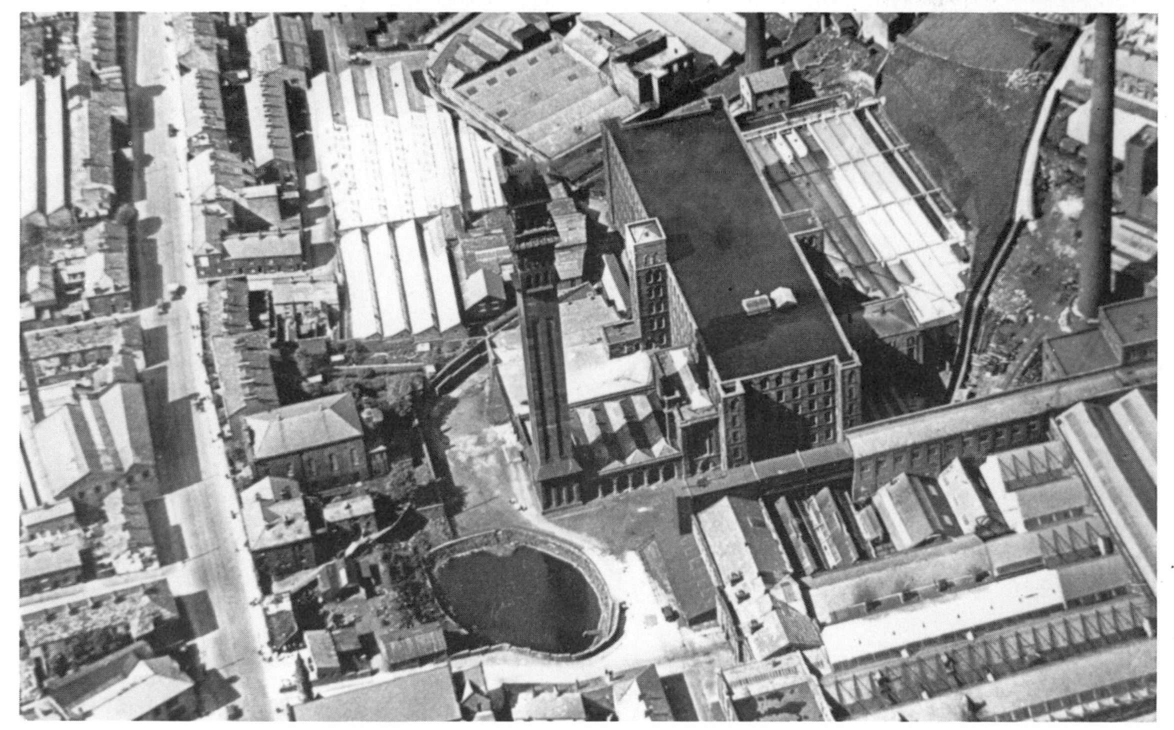

In Darwen, the Industrial Revolution came somewhat later than in Blackburn, and it was not until the 1830s that the large-scale development of the town and its industries really got under way. Darwen, though, has one of the great masterpieces of nineteenth-century British architecture, the celebrated India Mill chimney. Built in 1867, this 300-foot high triumph of engineering dominates the town and is a famous landmark, now preserved and cherished. The mill itself was situated on the bank of the River Darwen, and the winding course of the river can clearly be seen in this aerial view taken in 1939.

In all the mills fire was an ever-present danger. The abundance of highly-inflammable materials, the amount of waste fluff, often oil-soaked, and the wooden fittings and fixtures meant that, despite the development of fireproofing techniques and of fire-resistant building methods, outbreaks often occurred, some with spectacular and devastating consequences. This picture shows the fire at the India Mill, Darwen, on the fifteenth of June 1908.

***Right:** Dressed for a wedding. The interior of the India Mill, Haygarth Street, Blackburn, bedecked with streamers, ribbons, garlands and paper chains in celebration of a wedding in 1930. It is not known whose wedding was being celebrated.*

Gas supplies marked one of the major technological advances in urban areas in the nineteenth century, allowing, for the first time, full-scale street lighting and efficient domestic lighting as well as, later in the century, a new fuel for use in cooking. The town gasworks was a characteristic sight, but its interior is less familiar. This picture, taken about 1910, shows the retort room of the Green Bank gasworks, Blackburn. Had the floor just been swept for the benefit of the photographer, or was it really always as spick and span as this?

The Blackburn and Darwen areas had many small collieries from the sixteenth century onwards, but almost all of them had closed by 1914, the seams being thin and broken and the better reserves exhausted. One of the last to be sunk was the Hoddlesden Colliery, where the pit was dug in 1861. Some coal was found, but rich seams of high-quality fireclay were also encountered, and the mine soon became primarily a clay producer. It was this discovery which gave rise to Place's Hoddlesden Fireclay Works, producing specialised earthenware and related goods. The view was taken on the fourteenth of May 1932, and shows the small (but exceptionally heavy!) tubs of clay being unloaded at the shaft-top.

This picture shows the interior of Kirk & Co., shuttle and shuttle-tip manufacturers of Cob Wall, Blackburn, in about 1900. Amid the tangle of belt-driven lathes and other machinery it is possible to see, on the left, the piles of thick branches and small tree trunks which were the raw material, with stacks of semi-finished wooden blocks, and, on the right, boxes neatly arranged containing the finished products. Small industrial concerns such as this were just as important to the local economy as the great mills, but their fortunes rose and fell in tandem with those of the latter. If the cotton industry suffered, so, immediately, did the many traders who supplied its needs.

Crook & Thompson, coal merchants, still used a horse and cart in the late 1920s when this photograph was taken. Their methods – wide, flat shovels, hand-sorting and grading, two-wheeled coal barrows and a two-wheeled horse cart – were traditional for generations, but the motor lorry and mechanical sorting and loading were soon to bring dramatic changes and to make this a scene of the past.

Engineering and iron-founding were industries of the East Lancashire towns, developing originally using small local iron-ore deposits, and later expanding to meet the demands for engineering products from the textile industry. The Darwen & Mostyn Ironworks was situated on the northern edge of Darwen, at Goose House Bridge. The works closed in 1930 but this view was taken six years ealier and shows the moulding of the pig-iron in troughs on the foundry floor, casting it to make the rough shapes of parts for machinery. The dirty, dangerous and often primitive conditions in the smaller ironworks and foundries are very apparent from this photograph.

At the end of a working life the fate of many was poverty. Those who became destitute, and whose families could not (or would not) support them, often had no choice – the authorities might remove them to the hated workhouse. Darwen workhouse was built at the beginning of the nineteenth century, and in 1837 was reported to have space for 500 inmates. There were other local workhouses serving the townships of Blackburn, Mellor, Lower Darwen and Livesey, and the five had a total of 1,276 places. Eventually, the central workhouse for the whole district was built at Blackburn (now Queen's Park Hospital), but the Darwen workhouse, shown here, was not demolished until the 1950s, despite being condemned as inadequate a century earlier!

House and home

I was born in 1901, into an incredibly insanitary world. The 'loo', called a closet or privy, was in the yard or at the bottom of the garden ('going' was an ordeal in bad weather: if it was blowing a gale and freezing cold you might hesitate and wonder if your journey was really necessary). At night you had a candle stuck in a glass jam jar to light the way down the yard. In the outside toilet, torn-up newspaper hung on a nail behind the door, and a removeable tub was the only 'facility', emptied about once a month by a gang of so-called 'midnight mechanics'. Visitors to your house accepted the outside toilet as a normal arrangement – most of them had them too!

There was a chamber-pot under every bed or in a bedside cupboard. Elderly people would have a night commode in the bedroom. Some of the chambers were embossed with beautifully coloured floral designs and were quite expensive – they are now collectors' items. Another feature of the bedroom was the marble-topped dressing table with a large porcelain water jug and basin and a soap dish. A folded towel was usually kept on a rail on the side of the table (but the water, of course, would have to be carried up the stairs).

Bath night was a tin bath in front of the kitchen fire, with a lot of

Almost all terraced houses had an outdoor lavatory or privy, and only in the late-nineteenth century did provision of indoor 'facilities' start to be a regular feature of housing plans. Many houses often shared a privy with neighbours, and generally this involved common use of a long rear yard or passage. This is a row of three such common privies behind houses in Wellington Street, Darwen, in 1925.

carbolic soap. Pears' soap, as widely advertised by the picture of 'Bubbles', was as yet something of a luxury. All the family took a dip in the bath in turn – the last one had cold, dirty water. To dry her hair, a woman would lie on the hearth rug with her head resting near the fender.

Washday was a dolly-tub and heavy wringers, and a rack which was suspended from the ceiling on which to air clothes.

In the winter time a brick was kept in the oven, and just before

For many thousands of people housing conditions were deplorable. This was the consequence of the rapid industrial and urban growth, the lack of any sanitary provision, and the inability of local action to tackle the huge problems. In Blackburn and Darwen the ever-increasing population crammed into old and insanitary cottages and courts, at incredibly high densities. This view shows Bolton's Court, Richmond Terrace, Blackburn, in 1925. Rough and irregular paving, leaning walls and gables, and little or no sanitation were typical of such places. In areas such as Blackburn there were often half-cellars, with steps down, which were used as dwellings or which had been weavers' shops in the days of the handloom. The steps to the door of the house above were often an indication of such cellars.

bedtime it was wrapped in an old blanket and put into your bed. That was an ideal bedwarmer – an early storage heater, in effect – and it kept its warmth most of the night. Children were given a candle to light the way to bed as the moving shadows were very frightening.

By 1905 a start was made in building a better type of terraced house, each with its own separate water supply and a proper w.c. – though still outside. Some even had a tiny bathroom in the space over the stairs, and a very few had bay windows too! Looking back on those earlier

Housing conditions in the late-eighteenth-century and early-nineteenth-century districts of Blackburn, dating from the early years of the Industrial Revolution, were already recognised as a disgrace by the 1870s, particularly on the grounds of grossly inadequate sanitation. In 1879 Blackburn Corporation promoted a private Act of Parliament, dealing with a wide range of municipal matters, among them powers to tackle slum clearance, unfit housing and sanitary improvements. As part of the evidence to be presented to Parliament these and a series of other photographs were taken. They show (above) the back lane between the ironically-named Paradise Street and High Street, Lower Darwen, and (below) the rear of the south side of High Street, Lower Darwen. The shocking conditions are amply demonstrated. The slate-roofed 'sheds' or extensions occupying most of the tiny backyards are the ash-pit privies, not much more than their name suggests and emptied very infrequently, usually when the foul contents overflowed. The lanes seem to be full of mounds of such ash and other noxious refuse, and clearly were not cleaned at all.

The 1879 Act was also intended to deal with housing, which could be condemned on the grounds of unfitness for human habitation. This was a power which might be used where a property was in a physically dangerous state, as many were. Another photograph from the 1879 evidence shows occupied housing in Salford, Blackburn, and illustrates well the crazy angles and precarious condition of inner-urban housing in the town.

Greggs Gardens, Darwen (off South Road and Back High Street) was an area of eighteenth-century housing in the very centre of the town, and it predated the industrial and urban development of the town. By 1925 it was regarded as insanitary, and this photograph shown was taken in advance of clearance. The rough stone construction again marks these as eighteenth-century properties as in the nineteenth century dressed stone and, in some parts, brick were the standard materials. This is the sort of housing which would have been found in a village in the eighteenth century – and at that time Darwen was indeed a small village.

days it is amazing how people endured the unhygienic and difficult conditions.

There were four fireplaces in the new houses, one in the living room, another in the parlour and two in bedrooms upstairs. There was nothing to equal a glowing fire to warm the house, but it had its disadvantages. Coal had to be delivered to the back yard and then shovelled into a shed, you needed sticks to light the fire (and in the middle of town you just couldn't go out and gather them) and at least once a day the ashes had to be raked out and taken to the ash bin. A fair amount of rubbish was burned on the open fire grates and occasionally the soot would catch fire which was an alarming experience; red hot lumps of soot would fall down into the fireplace and sometimes spill out onto the hearth. Often when this happened the fire brigade would have to be called out and they would climb into the roof and sprinkle water down the chimney – and that was another mess to clean up.

They used to say 'A woman's work is never done', and that was all

These two views of Wellington Street (top) and Union Street, Darwen, were taken in 1925 and 1934 respectively, and show early- and mid-nineteenth century housing, dating from the time of Darwen's great growth into a town and a major centre of industry. The regularly-shaped stone used for building indicates the change which has taken place since the houses in the previous picture were built. Housing of the type shown here represented a great improvement upon older types, in many senses, but still lacked many of the features which we regard as commonplace and essential.

too true. A proud housewife would black-lead all the iron parts of the kitchen range about once a week and the brass fender, shovel, poker and tongs would be polished until they shone in the firelight. An indication of a clean house and a well-kept house was a clean doorstep, and one of the first jobs in the morning was to mop it and donkey-stone the top edge. There was usually a rag-and-bone man shouting in the back streets for any old rags and bones or pieces of old iron, in exchange for which he would give you a donkey stone.

One day a week - perhaps Thursday - was baking day. When you went to school in the morning there was a great big earthenware mug full of dough on the hearth and when you came home in the afternoon the dining room and kitchen were covered with bread and barmcakes. There were mounds of golden-brown scones, a big tin of parkin and oven-bottom cakes (a sort of scone) to be eaten with lashings of fresh butter and streams of golden syrup. You looked forward to these special occasions and you ran all the way home from school. Sometimes a man would come to your door selling oatcakes, which he took out of a basket balanced on his head.

In the old grandma's kitchen there was a copper boiler which was built round with stone or brick and had a chimney of the same material. Under it a fire grate used to heat up the water in the boiler. Monday was washday, and the weekly washing was boiled up in it, but on other days, and at least once a week, the boiler was swilled out and filled with broth; cabbages, peas, carrots, lentils, barley and onions and then a big sheep's head was dropped into it. A loud rattle of pots in the yard brought children from round about, all running to get their tin mugs and pint pots full of that savoury stew. That was 'owd grandma's' special treat for them.

People who before the Industrial Revolution lived in the country, and perhaps had mixed with gypsies, had gathered a smattering of knowledge as to the curative healing qualities of various herbs, some of which grew freely in the countryside. There were various superstitions and old wives' remedies concerning disease and childbirth. Coloured beads or sometimes a gold chain placed around a baby's neck were supposed to ward off evil spirits, to keep the child free from disease and help in the easy cutting of the child's teeth. Cinder tea was a good remedy for wind in babies - a white-hot cinder was dropped into half a cup of water and a little sugar added before the child drank it. An old cure for rickets was to take the child out and roll it in the long, dewy grass, rub it briskly with a hot towel and put on a red flannel vest. A dock leaf rubbed on a nettle sting would take the pain away and a spider's web wrapped round a cut finger would stop the bleeding and heal it without festering. A nutmeg carried in the pocket would help to keep you free from 'rheumatic acid', and the nauseous springtime tonic of 'sulphur and treacle' was said to be good for you as it would cleanse the blood (No, you didn't rub it in, you drank the ...... stuff off a tablespoon!).

When you were ill you were kept off school. If you had a sore throat you had a slice of bacon tied round your neck, a troublesome cough was likely to be rubbed with goose grease and whooping cough required a much more drastic treatment - one remedy was for a child to be given a fried or boiled mouse to eat.

Left: *The tightly-packed terraces of mid-nineteenth century housing, overshadowed by towering mill buildings and chimneys – the cathedrals of the Industrial Age – are shown in this view of Larkhill, taken about 1930. Almost all of this area has since been cleared and redeveloped, and few recognisable landmarks now remain. Regent Street runs from left to right along the bottom of the picture, and Victoria Street runs in at an angle from the left hand side, about halfway up.*

This shows part of Waterfall and Green Park, taken, like the Larkhill view, on a flight over Blackburn about 1930. Mill Hill railway station is in the lower left hand corner, and the two courses of the River Darwen can be seen.

A good story is told of a tackler who lived in Clitheroe whose wife had been rather out of sorts, so she went to see her doctor:

'I think you have some slight kidney trouble', he said. 'However, take plenty of barley water'.

The good wife told her husband what the doctor had prescribed and the next day he set off for Barley (in the Pendle district) with two buckets and brought back the essential 'barley water'!

It was fairly well known that there was no better remedy than comfrey for consumption or for chest and lung trouble. In the early part of the century epsom salts were sold by the ton load, and it also became common to give children a spoonful of castor oil at least once a week. For a severe chill the patient was given a mustard bath, rolled in a blanket and put to bed to sweat it out. You could tell if there was a case of pneumonia in your street as a cart load of ashes would be spread over the cobblestones to deaden the sound of horses and carts passing by. The neighbours spoke quietly of the time when the 'crisis' would take place. Some of the older people will remember having syrup of figs, or perhaps brimstone and treacle. The mother of a family would, now and then, mix a handful of senna-pods with the tea in the teapot (ya!).

School and education

BY a deed of 1512, Thomas Stanley, second Earl of Derby and lord of a neighbouring manor, provided for a grammar school for the people of Blackburn. After a petition by the inhabitants the school was granted a royal charter and was subsequently known as the Free Grammar School of Queen Elizabeth. It was said that the sons of some of the best families in Blackburn, Darwen and the neighbourhood were sent to the Blackburn Grammar School! Some of the boys who came from Darwen walked the four miles, sometimes in the dark, to be present at 7 a.m., and then returned home after 5 p.m.. There were sections of the route which were very lonely indeed, and the fertile imaginations of eleven- and twelve-year-old boys were full of thieves and ghosts! The school continued to grow with the town and in 1974 began to admit girls into the sixth form.

When I was young schools did not suffer from vandalism and graffiti as we know them today. With a policeman in your district, walking along your street at all hours of the night and day – maybe even living in your own or in a neighbouring street – you had to be well-behaved. He would know of you and who you were, and even worse, he would know your father. If at times you were inclined to be a little devil there was, in some homes, a leather strap hanging on the wall . . .

But punishment like that was meted out frequently at school, too; the principle of education often seemed to be that the brain would only absorb what the backside could stand in punishment. Looking back on his school days in Blackburn a nearly ninety-year-old said that all children wore clogs, which in the early morning had to be clean or else you were for it. He recalled that one little chap when asked what he was called always replied, 'I'm the king of the muck-tubs', which set all the other children laughing helplessly. The teachers soon found out

The foundation stone of the Blackburn Ragged School in Bent Street was laid in 1885. The school was the product of the philanthropy, and the social conscience, of two local men, John T. Walkden and James Dixon. They had been deeply moved by the sight and the plight of hundreds of destitute, homeless vagrant and neglected children who wandered the streets of mid-nineteenth-century Blackburn. In 1875, for example, it was reported that over a quarter of the children of school age did not go to school, primarily because they were destitute. The Ragged School, by offering food, clothing, shelter and the rudiments of education to thousands of such children, did sterling work.

The view of the prize band, one of the star attractions of the school, was taken in 1896. This is a procession of the boys of St. Stephen's School, Blackburn, on their Field Day about 1905.

that it was no use smacking him, he just couldn't help it.

Another boy drank ink out of the ink wells. Unruly children were sometimes severely punished and on the odd occasion a boy might be frog-marched and pushed into a coal hole and left in the pitch darkness and the door would be fastened from the outside. There was a farmer's boy who was always late for school and when asked why this was so, cheekily replied, 'I've been kittin' milk'. The headmaster thought the time had come to teach the lad a lesson and began to thrash him with a cane. However, the lad was big for his years and he butted the master and knocked him down, then sat on him and started hitting *him* with clenched fists! There was 'such a carry-on as never was'. The teachers ran to the master's assistance while the children in the other classrooms stood on their desks looking through the glass partitions and cheered them on.

In the mornings the glass partitions were pushed against the wall. The headmaster said a prayer and then everyone, accompanied by his squeaky violin, joined together in singing a hymn. He seemed, quite unfairly, to pick on someone and in a monotone sang 'Smith (or Jones!) - you - are - out - of - tune - go - into - the - corridor - and - I'll - see - you - later'. A few minutes later he would look at you, evidently puzzled as to why you were standing there, and then he would smile in a kindly sort of way and say, 'Tell you father to pay for you to have some singing lessons'.

There was a geography master at that school who was a well-known cricketer. He had a nasty habit of throwing the duster (a padded piece of wood for cleaning the blackboard) at an inattentive scholar. He never hit the one he aimed at, but had a fair amount of explaining to do to the mothers of innocent and aggrieved (or even bruised) scholars.

Playtime was your own precious time – time to run and shout and go wild, or maybe to stand and stare. The girls worked off their energy by skipping. They skipped with a good long rope and sang or chanted a jingle for their game:

'Whom shall I marry: Tinker, tailor, soldier, sailor, rich man, poor man, beggarman, thief?'

Continuing with:

'What shall I wear: Silk, satin, muslin, rags!'

'What shall I ride in: Coach, carriage, wheelbarrow, muck-cart?'

The game ended as the rope twirled faster and faster and they all called out:

'Salt, vinegar, mustard, pepper'.

Rounders was another game which was played by boys and girls alike, with great vigour. There was a great shout of triumph when someone on your side reached the den without being caught or hit.

To miss school for only a few days would bring the dreaded school board officer knocking loudly on the door and threatening to summons parents if there was not a good and sufficient reason for their child's absence.

There didn't seem to be any weeding out of 'unteachable' children. The backward, neglected or mentally handicapped were all there. It was very unfortunate for any left-handed children, though, as they were considered to be awkward and were frequently punished for it.

There had been a very low standard of education prior to 1900, but by the time of the Great War children coming off the school 'production lines', with the leaving age then thirteen and a half or fourteen years, would have gained a reasonable standard. This meant that they had more opportunities for finding a variety of better jobs; apprentices in industries, tramway parcels delivery services, telegram service, errand boys and, in the case of girls, shop assistants, clerks and shorthand typists. The drudgery of domestic service was fast disappearing.

But still, after a normal and long day's work, from six in the morning until six in the evening in many jobs, you cast off your overalls, cleaned up and then joined hundreds and hundreds of others in going to night school. Your education was still not finished, even though you had ended your schooldays.

Praise and pray

IN the early years of the century there was an upsurge of religious fervour. Almost everybody 'belonged' to some church or chapel which, especially on 'Sermon's' Sundays boasted of large congregations and remarkably large 'collections'.

St. Silas's Church, in Blackburn, was a very fashionable place of worship. On Sunday mornings it was attended by the cotton manufacturers and the brewers. The Coddingtons, the Birtwistles, the Harrisons, the Nutalls and their wives knelt in their own pews. Huge picture hats, frock coats and tall hats (shiners) were the order of the day for the gentry.

The experiences and impressions we gain when we are young are often carried through to adulthood and remain for the rest of our lives. To be a choir boy and to take part in such oratorios as Sphore's *Last Judgement*, Stainer's *Crucifixion* and, of course, Handel's *Messiah* was to receive great joy and satisfaction, and is just such a memory. It was a very great honour to be chosen to sing the solo part 'Oh! for the wings of a dove, faraway would I rove; in the wilderness build me a nest, and remain there forever at rest'.

There was very little to do in the long, dark evenings, without radio or television. To people with good singing voices the church choirs were a great attraction, and occasionally different churches would hold choir festivals, when, with choirs from several churches all together, and accompanied by an orchestra of local musicians, they would ambitiously and (usually) very successfully perform oratorios such as these. On those great occasions it would have been possible to display the 'House Full' notices on the doors.

The initiation of a new boy into the choir was a lesson in man's inhumanity to man, and another of those memories which are never forgotten. The new boy was sneered at and insulted, rolled over and over on the ground in his best Sunday suit, and finally pushed over a

The ancient parish church of St. Mary the Virgin, Blackburn, was once the focus of a huge parish which extended as far as Walton-le-Dale, Langho and Darwen. The building was completely reconstructed in the 1820s and then again after a fire in the 1830s. In 1926 the church was chosen as the cathedral to serve the newly-created diocese of Blackburn, and a series of ambitious plans for enlargement were drawn up, although some were later cancelled, and building work has continued almost up to the present day. In this view the distinctive square tower of the parish church, in pre-cathedral days, forms a characteristic backdrop to a view of the Boulevard, with a selection of horse-drawn hansom cabs and four-wheeled 'growlers', in about 1905.

St. Silas's Church, one of Blackburn's many places of worship dating from the nineteenth-century expansion of the town, was in the early years of this century regarded as particularly fashionable, and was attended by the cotton manufacturers, the brewers, their families and servants. It was also attended by the author of this book who was a choirboy there and who was later a member of the St. Silas's Church Lads Brigade.

six-foot wall.

To the choir boys the annual picnic was the highlight of the year. The favourite destination was Southport where a day out for the choir included boating in the botanical gardens and a 'nosh-up' in a *real* café (with side plates). Before leaving Blackburn the boys had bought for themselves a packet of cigarettes – Woodbines were a firm favourite at three pence for ten; another favourite was 'Blue Book'. These were in packets of ten different tobaccos – Virginia, Russian, Turkish and Egyptian were some of them. Some of the more experienced and daring lads, with more pocket money, bought a packet of 'Miranda's Dreams', an exotically scented cigarette with a gold band. On one choir picnic most of the boys were riding on the top of a tram in Lord Street, Southport, the choir master and the vicar were sitting inside. The word went round that the boys were to be searched for cigarettes and there was a cascade of cigarettes and packets from the top of the tram into Lord Street – to the passers-by it must have seemed like cigarettes from heaven!

At this time the Church Army was prominent in holding 'Revival' meetings in the church halls, and, like the Salvation Army, could always be found holding services and meetings on the sands of the holiday resorts. The Evangelical sections of the Church of England held an annual summer convention at Keswick in Cumberland and, being in a neighbouring county, this event was very popular with devout Lancashire churchgoers – it could be thought of as a holiday too. The religious services were held in enormous marquees, whilst groups of people held prayer and discussion meetings in every nook and corner of the town.

Shops and shopping

N 1844 some poor weavers in Rochdale launched the modern consumers' co-operative movement when they opened their small shop in Toad Lane. The Rochdale pioneers laid down the principles on which co-operative enterprises could be conducted and they popularised the 'dividend', and thereafter all societies followed their example.

But, there were many people who thought that the opening of a shop themselves would put them on 'easy street', and that those who were struggling to make ends meet would solve their problems by this means. Many became obsessed with the idea and small corner shops, mostly selling food, began to appear in side streets in all the towns. In turn, the town centre shops became larger, brighter, cleaner and better lit, and their goods were more attractively and enticingly displayed.

In Blackburn, Johnny Forbes, the famous Blackburn Rovers left-back, opened his gentleman's outfitters shop. Beatty Brothers, the tailors in Church Street and Tills, the tailors in Two Gates, offered boy's sailor suits in serges and tweeds from two shillings and eleven pence (fourteen new pence), men's ready-to-wear Norfolk suits from twenty-one shillings (one pound, five new pence) and cycling suits from fifteen shillings and eleven pence (seventy-nine new pence). Between 1880 and 1900 the Co-operative and multiple stores expanded enormously.

The great Marks and Spencers came to Darwen Street, Blackburn, in all humility. They had started on Leeds market in 1884, by the end of 1900, had thirty-six branches and had planted an acorn from which a very great forest of oak trees was to grow. But in the early years they sold mainly from market stalls – twenty-four of the thirty-six outlets in 1900 were in market halls – and their hallmark was cheapness. In Blackburn there was no fanfare of trumpets or civic reception to greet them on the opening of the Penny Bazaar. Instead, on the counters were notices saying 'Don't ask the price – it's a penny!'

Looking back, it is unbelievable to see the immense range of household goods sold in Marks and Spencers Penny Bazaar. There were skeins of wool, black and white reels of cotton, bundles of elastic (for making garters for concertina stockings and for keeping up 'unmentionables'). There were corset laces (double strength to stand a knee in the back and the pull of two strong arms!), hairpins, safety pins, buttons, darning needles, knitting needles, brooches, combs and handkerchiefs. There were envelopes, writing pads, ink and note books – don't ask the price – it's a penny.

In one tray there would be eight varieties of biscuits in sealed packets, and wrapped bars of chocolate and toffee. In another tray you would find nails, screws, chisels, hammers and corkscrews. And for the kitchen there would be pan lids, cake tins, cups and saucers, pudding bowls and basins, dish cloths, boot polish, soap, soap powder, matches and many other items. For the children there were toys, tin and wooden engines, wooden dolls, lead soldiers, rattles, picture books, slates and pencils, tinsels and baubles. Don't ask the price – it's a penny.

In these days of the mighty dollar and the devalued pound, let us spare a thought for the 'Almighty penny'. A penny was the usual weekly spending money for many thousands of children – the 'Saturday penny', if they were lucky enough to have anything at all. A penny really was a penny in those days – it would buy thirty aniseed balls or a bar of chocolate. From penny-in-the-slot machines you could be told your weight or your fortune, you could get five Woodbines or a bar of 'Five Boys' chocolate. At the railway station you got a penny platform ticket if you were meeting someone off the train, or if perhaps you were with a party of wedding guests to see the bride and groom off on their honeymoon. A diversion: for a tip of sixpence, a porter would lock the door of their confetti-smothered compartment to avoid their being disturbed. As all porters carried a key to fit the door locks there would be no difficulty in getting out at their destination, usually 'the West coast' – the posh name for Blackpool! There were penny slot machines on the doors of public toilets; everybody knew what the whispered 'to spend a penny' meant. That expression and a great many others gained a not insignificant place in our language.

There was great encouragement to 'do it yourself' in the shops and many people, of course, had no choice in the matter – do it yourself or don't have it done. For a few coppers, dressmaking was within every woman's reach. The women in the churches and chapels began their sewing classes, and soon they were mending and patching and making better, and sometimes making clothes from new for the family.

Shops were exciting and sometimes mysterious places, full of fascination for children. It was a delight to be sent to the grocer's on an errand as the bell on the shop door gave out a merry tinkle and immediately you entered a wonderful world of exotic perfumes – newly-ground coffee, spices, nutmeg and succulent hams. There were rolls of bacon and gammon, cured in brine and hanging from the ceiling on great hooks; there was freshly baked bread and great tubs of butter; there was candied peel and sacks of flour and oatmeal.

The grocer and his wife and buxom daughters in white aprons would weigh the sugar and pack it in blue paper bags. They patted butter into oblong shapes, wrapping it skilfully and quickly to keep it cool, fresh and clean. The grocer's son, hurrying about, carried baskets full of orders to the pony and van which were standing at the kerb

This extremely early photograph of the centre of Darwen, although damaged, gives an excellent idea of the character of the town before the building of public offices and shops in the 1870s and 1880s. The picture is thought to have been taken in 1864, and shows Holy Trinity Church, built in 1829, with its 'handsome tower' dominating the scene. Darwen's oldest church was St. James's, which dated in origin from the sixteenth century, although rebuilt in 1853. The scene shows Darwen almost as a country village, which it had been half a century before this photograph was taken.

Pickering's, the brushmakers, of 37 Church Street, Blackburn, was a very old-established Blackburn firm. The photograph was taken about 1875 and shows the shop, founded in 1825 by Peter Pickering. It was a very old buildings, although the medieval-style castellations on the front were not original! Behind the shop was a three-storey showroom and warehouse, and also the brush works itself. This firm was highly regarded, and a large trade was done with mills and shopkeepers, farmers and gentry, the latter being large buyers of the firm's brushes for use in the stables.

waiting to deliver.

The shop would be open until eight o'clock at night, lit in the darker months by the mysterious warm glow from the oil lamps. But now your shopping bag would have been packed and it was full and almost too heavy for a small boy to carry. A big piece of treacle toffee would be pushed into your mouth as you searched through your pockets for the money to pay for what you had ordered. Two enormous mouse-catchers would be chased out of the way and usually you would be told to jump up behind the horse if the boy was going your way to deliver the groceries. The total cost for a basketful of groceries? About three shillings - fifteen pence in today's money!

Above: *All self-respecting towns in Yorkshire and Lancashire built shopping arcades in the late nineteenth century, and of course, Blackburn was no exception. This view, taken about 1900, shows Thwaites Arcade, looking at the entrance in Lord Street. Like such arcades in more recent times, it housed speciality shops and in 1889, for example, included at No. 4, W. H. Cunliffe's artists' materials store, a sign of the sophistication that had come to nineteenth century Blackburn as its prosperity and cultural provision grew.*

Right: *Darwen Street and Blackburn Cathedral, 1929. The old parish church had just become the cathedral, but as yet there had been no start on the extensions which would so greatly alter the building in ensuing years. The old shops in Darwen Street, some already empty and due for demolition, must have been built in the eighteenth century, if not before.*

On the market

MY father had inherited a fruit business on Blackburn market. When the 1914-18 war was over, other countries with better and warmer climates than ours, or with specialist market-gardening industries, began to export produce and wakened to the fact that they could compete with English growers. We started to sell lettuces from Denmark and France, potatoes and tomatoes from Jersey and Guernsey and, of course, tulips from Amsterdam. There were many benefits to be gained at our end from this new venture, with fresh salad produce. It would be necessary to buy direct from the importers, and many of these were based on Shudehill market in Manchester. I was enrolled as a junior member of the firm and straightaway we ordered a Ford lorry, an old Tin Lizzy, from Walshes on Northgate – the cost was about ninety-eight pounds. I got a driving licence for five bob (no questions asked), and in two weeks the lorry was all painted up and fresh with 'Ben Forrest *& Son*' across its side, and ready for collection. The tank was full of petrol. I was given a starting handle to wind it up and told how to set the ignition lever. I had never driven or ridden anything on the road except a push bike and I had never felt so lonely in my life.

There were no restrictions whatsoever, except, of course, that a sidelight had to be shown on the off-side, and a red lamp at the back – and the driver had to recognise and obey lighting-up time. Otherwise, nothing. No rules – and no instruction.

Market stalls in open-air markets have changed little since 1906 when this picture of Hartley's fruit and vegetable stall on Blackburn market was taken. The stalls were of canvas and wood and were dismantled and re-erected twice a week. Perhaps the price labels, if we could read them, might cause some wry amusement today. The greatest change between then and now might be the much wider variety and range of produce which we would now see on such a stall.

The market in Blackburn was one of the largest in nineteenth-century Lancashire, tracing its origins back at least to the sixteenth century and probably before. It and the cattle fairs were originally held on the waste ground at Blakey Moor, before the formal market place was laid out in the 1850s. It drew customers and traders from all over East Lancashire, but was a particular magnet for the Ribble Valley and the lower Darwen/Calder valleys. This picture was taken about 1906, and shows Victoria Street on market day (either Wednesday or Saturday). The streets appear to have been swept, as later in the day they would be covered in dirt and market refuse and fouled with horse manure.

On the market there were no refrigerators like there are now, and in hot weather meat, fish, poultry, soft fruits and any other perishables were auctioned off late on Saturday night. Lots of people did most of their shopping then and bought their Sunday dinner for a few coppers. Blackburn market in the early-1920s was a very busy and very noisy place. There always seemed to be crowds of people walking about while the stallholders shouted their wares at the tops of their voices. Horses and carts were there delivering fruit and vegetables, hansom cabs passed to and fro along King William Street and noisy, clanking trams came up the road between the stalls and the town hall. In the cinemas there were two houses shown on Saturday night, and after the first house ended at 8.30 p.m. the centre of the town was alive with people walking about, and the market hall was filled to capacity.

The stalls were made with wooden frames covered with canvas sheets. They had to be erected very early on market days and taken down again late at night ready to be stored away in the market hall cellars. The market was open on Wednesday and Saturday, and like the shops the market hall was open until 8 p.m. on Wednesday, and even later – 9 p.m. – on Saturday. The markets attracted all sorts of men for this and other sorts of labouring. There was 'strong Dick', an odd-job man on the market about 1910. He grew dissatisfied and let it be known that he intended to 'get out of it' – he thought he would walk around the world, for a change, he said. Sure enough, one morning he was in the centre of a large crowd who slapped him on the back, made a collection for him and cheered as he strode away on the main road. But, to everyone's surprise, there he was, back at work on the following market day – he had turned back at Bolton!

In a covered stall on the market, furnished with a trestle table and two forms, you could sit down and eat a couple of black puddings with lashings of mustard. You could go to another stall and have a plate full of tripe. There was something for everybody; a little pet rabbit would cost you sixpence (two and a half new pence) and, on the poultry stall, duck eggs were very common.

The land to the south of the River Ribble was the market garden for East Lancashire, despite the growing foreign competition from imported salad produce. Wagons drawn by horses brought loads of potatoes, carrots, lettuce, cabbages, cauliflowers, sprouts, celery and soft fruits from the market gardens at Hesketh Bank, Longton, Banks, Ormskirk, Penwortham, Walton-le-Dale and Tarleton. The wagons would gather at the Halfway House on the Preston to Blackburn new road on Thursday night. This long wagon train rumbled and shrieked as it came down Preston New Road for Blackburn market at 5 a.m. on a Friday, waking everybody in the roadside houses.

The fruit and vegetable merchants were housed in substantial timber-built fruit stalls on the Victoria Street side of the old market hall and fish market. To handle all the fruit and vegetables coming in for Blackburn and the surrounding districts was itself big business. The wholesale fruiterers were well respected and ran solid, financially sound businesses. In one office you could see a photograph of the steamer in which the 'boss' had sailed to the Canary Islands, and in another, a photograph of a Fyffes banana boat on which the banana merchant from Blackburn had sailed as a guest of that famous company.

To the Darwen Market

MY father had decided to retire and, as there was a movement afoot to transfer the whole of the Blackburn Market to a new site, with no possibility of being able to sell the business, I decided to make a complete break with the old, and soon I was doing something more ambitious and more in keeping with my nature.

With my Sunday School prizes, I opened a book stall in Darwen Market Hall. On that first day, I could hardly have realised that I would still be there thirty-five years later!

As soon as I was settled there, and the business was firmly established, I began to take a greater interest in local affairs and, during the ensuing years, I became an active member in such worthy organisations as the Booksellers' Association, the Blackburn Ramblers' Association, the Blackburn Artists' Society (the Blackburn Technical College), the Blackburn Philosophical and Scientific Society, the Darwen Chamber of Trade, the Darwen Arts Council, the Darwen Literary Society and, for no less than forty-five years, the

***Top:** The Market Hall at Darwen was built in 1885 by the new Corporation (the town had been incorporated as a borough in 1878). Hitherto, there had been an informal open-air market, although as a latecomer to the towns of Lancashire, Darwen did not have a market tradition as did Blackburn. The site chosen for the new market was a difficult one. It needed a good wide expanse of level ground and there was very little of that available in the centre of Darwen that was not already occupied. The answer was to use the bottom of the valley of the River Darwen, which was covered over for a further stretch, and to add the site of an old watermill dam and pond, which were demolished and drained and then levelled for the purpose. This rare photograph, probably taken about 1880, shows the site of the market hall before the draining and filling-in work. It is difficult to recognise that this view shows the heart of modern Darwen!*

Darwen's new municipal buildings and market hall were the first major piece of imposing architecture in the town, apart from its churches, and they were deliberately designed to be a centrepiece to the town centre, then undergoing a lot of development and improvement. The photograph must have been taken in the 1890s, as there is no clock as yet provided on the clockface of the tower – the clock was eventually put in place in 1900.

Darwen Rotary Club.

Darwen market was quite different from Blackburn market, but just as busy and just as noisy. When it was opened, over a century ago, it was more like a covered cattle market than the clean, orderly shopping places we know today, displaying on its bright, well-kept stalls almost everything you might need from your weekly shopping list. It was originally a place where the farmers and growers could sell live pigs, geese, turkeys, ducks and hens, and farm produce – butter, eggs, cheese, fruit and vegetables. The toll for taking a cartload of mixed vegetables into the market was remarkably low – only one shilling (five new pence). The horse and cart would be driven into the hall, selling would take place from the cart, and the horse taken away until the time came to return home.

In a guide book published in 1920, Darwen was said to be an uninteresting cotton town amongst the hills, but by the 1930s there had been great improvements to the trade of the town, and the market had become well established and of some consequence. Many important firms of high repute and long standing had become traders in the town but, unfortunately, the whole of Darwen was very badly hit by the terrible depression of the early-1930s. With very little money about and so few customers, the young assistants in the market hall found very little to do except on market days, so they played table tennis, setting up a table for this in one of the passages. There was even a dancing class, but as musical instruments were not allowed to be played in the market hall, it was necessary to wait until the market superintendent went to his dinner before bringing the wind-up gramophone out of its hiding place! Then it was time for 'Knees up Mother Brown' and 'Choose your partner for the next dance'.

All this merriment was actually good for trade as people came in from elsewhere in the town during their lunch break to watch or join in the fun, whilst others came to watch and buy from the stalls. This worked very well to the benefit of all concerned, until a sour-faced manageress from a multiple store (both the manageress and the store now long gone), who wore a black dress trailing to the floor and stood straight as a ram-rod in lace-up boots, reported the matter to the market superintendent. The gramophone was confiscated by order of the market clerk.

Saturday night in the market hall, as at Blackburn, was always a social occasion. When the first house at the cinema finished at 8.30 p.m. everybody flocked into the market hall which was very busy indeed. In the 1920s and '30s, Darwen gained a reputation as a prosperous market town and, remarkably, even Blackpool landladies organised coach trips to Darwen for a day out to see the market.

There were some bitterly cold winters in the 1930s, and it was perishing cold in the market hall, with its two-inch gap under the ill-fitting doors and no installed heating. In those days the tenants were held in disfavour by the borough council, several members of which were shop owners in the High Street; they thought that too prosperous and too comfortable a market hall would be to their disadvantage. In all meetings with the markets committee and the borough council, the stallholders were expected to go 'cap in hand'. To commemorate the occasion for 'begging for heating', someone was inspired to write a poem about what could well have happened under the circumstances. It has never been published and nobody else has seen it until now:

The Market Hall Rent Increase
1st August 1937

'A thousand pounds!' the Mayor looked blue,
so did the Corporation too.
A thousand pounds to warm the market,

'Why! does anyone go in it?
With great care let us decide
And study up our maths'.
Remember the public did deride
The layout on the baths!' (new swimming baths
Then up spoke one with very loud voice
(not unmixed with passion)
We'll give them warmth if it is their choice
But in quite another fashion.
The tenants then met in consultation
To beg for a little moderation
of this our Corporation;
'Come in!' the Mayor cried (looking bigger)
And in they went (not lacking vigour).
The tenants' compliments we present,
But regret that they resent
This large increase of twenty per cent
Come Sirs! this can never be meant.
Twenty per cent is out of proportion
To set this apparatus in motion.
The Mayor was dumb and the Council stood
as if they were changed into blocks of wood.
Could it be true what they could hear
These people telling them without fear?
But, the Councillors had it all off pat
We've made up our minds and that's that.
And as for the warmth, what we spoke
Of that, as you very well know, was no joke.
Losses we have made in plenty
Ten per cent would do, but let's say twenty'.

Albert Forrest
with apologies to Browning (Pied Piper)

It took a long time for the council to realise that the markets provided a service to the town and contributed a lot of money to the rates.

In the early days of the town the open-air market was situated in Belgrave Square until the new market ground and market hall were opened in 1881. This new position was ideal for its purpose. Surprisingly, in 1953, the town council considered a suggestion that the open-air market should be moved to the Atlas Mill site, or to the Old Peel baths premises, and that the market square should be laid out as a war memorial garden which would be moved from Bold Venture Park.

The Market Tenants Association told them that although a garden in the centre of Darwen would look very beautiful, it was quite unnecessary to replace an active market with something ornamental. The beauty of Darwen's parks and woods was unsurpassed in the whole of Lancashire and to provide gardens in the town centre would be – they said – rather to gild the lily.

Getting around

UNTIL the end of the First World War travelling was mostly by bicycle, by tram or by train – or, of course, by your own feet. In a copy of the *Blackburn Times* under the heading 'Cycling Notes' appeared the following:

'It was reported at the meeting that about fifty members of the Clarion Cycling Club opened the season on Sunday with a run to Myerscough Smithy. On Sunday, the members of the Ribblesdale Club went to Whalley and found the return journey against the strong wind a somewhat difficult job. Chester was the venue for the Clarion Easter meeting and the Crosshill Cycling Club made a brave show on their opening run of the season, the club being bound for Lytham. There was a creditable turn-out and all the members appeared on brand new machines.'

At a General Meeting of the Ribblesdale Cycling Club, 1898, Helen Waterson Moody said how cycling had modified ladies' dresses. They had been snipped and sheared and stitched and had come forth as a hybrid garment, neither male or female, lacking the sweet appeal of the flowing feminine line – lacking even the long petticoat, without which nobody could take them for women. Many of the lady members said they had been embarrassed by remarks shouted at them as they rode along. They had been called 'brazen hussies', and been told they were 'disgusting'. A frequent remark was 'Mind yer bloomers!'

There were many cycling clubs and if you were journeying on the roads you would meet about fifty or sixty cyclists taking up the full width of the road. You could turn a corner on a country lane and run smack into a herd of cattle being driven to market. The tram lines were a hazard in the town – if the wheels of your bike got caught in them you could suffer a nasty fall.

Long-distance cycling was not something I thought of on my early machines! If you wanted a new bicycle, if in fact you wanted anything at all, you had to save up for it out of your spending money, which was little enough. However, in families the bikes, like the clothes, were 'handed down'. So it came to pass that about the year 1912 I nearly met my doom at Billinge End, Blackburn, where only one motor car would pass through the crossroads about every quarter of an hour. Coming down Revidge Road the brakes on my rusty old handed-down bike would not hold. I went over the top and landed on the back seat of an open tourer which, by a happy coincidence, had chosen that moment to pass the crossroads. I picked myself up and looked at the buckled front wheel, and I felt sure that this was the end of my cycling days! But, my parents were so overjoyed that I hadn't been killed that they bought me a brand-new bike, complete with a saddle bag, pump, a tool kit, an acetylene lamp and good brakes – it's an ill wind, eh?

Much later, in the early-1920s, I bought a 1912 'Swift' motor car, and

Ribchester was a much-favoured destination for cycling excursions from Blackburn. These cyclists are out for the day in about 1905, attracted, no doubt, by the prospect of fresh air and fine scenery, with, at the end of the ride, an attractive old village with interesting antiquities, a pleasant riverside, several tea rooms and tea gardens and, for those who liked something a little stronger than tea, a selection of venerable and popular hostelries.

Even in 1922, when this picture of King William Street was taken, motor cars were still a rarity. There is just one car in the whole length of the street – such a lot of free parking space going to waste! However, rather eccentrically, the driver has parked six feet out from the kerb. Could it be the lady who is looking rather suspiciously . . . or in embarassment . . . at the camera? Since the pre-war photographs of the same street, seen earlier in this book, the road surface had been substantially altered, with a thin tarmacadam layer replacing, or more probably covering, the great stone setts of the earlier years.

in 1925 I drove it down to London to the British Empire Exhibition at Wembley. The speed limit in those days was twenty miles per hour and it was a long, slow journey. Apart from the driving licence, bought over the counter for five shillings (twenty-five new pence) and the number plates and paying the tax, which was one pound for each unit of horse-power, there were no restrictions. Except the twenty miles per hour speed limit! To get a licence to drive a car you had to be at least seventeen years old, or fourteen to ride a motorcycle.

It could be very dangerous motoring on the unlit country roads at night time with your headlamps giving a faint glimmer that could hardly penetrate the gloom, and no such things as windscreen wipers to help in wet weather. It had been known for motorists to be flagged down, when help was supposedly needed in a breakdown, and then to be attacked and robbed. Many drivers took the comfort of a thumping big spanner on the seat beside them, 'just in case'.

In the 1914-18 war a lot of motor vehicles were adapted to run off

The Blackburn Corporation horse trams were, in fact, not run by the Corporation itself, but by a private firm, confusingly named The Blackburn Corporation Tramways Company! Here we see tram no. 22, about 1895, at Billinge End, the terminus of the steeply graded route along Preston New Road from Salford Bridge. This route was the first to be converted to electric traction, when in 1899 the tramways were taken over directly by the Corporation.

The steam tram was a phenomenon particularly associated with the Pennine valley towns, where the great power of the steam locomotive at the front could haul a full tramcar up steep roads which would have been difficult or impossible for horses. This tram is seen in about 1900 on the Blackburn Corporation Tramways route from Salford Bridge to the Cemetery, along Whalley New Road.

domestic gas because of the shortage of petrol. The old town hall, Blackburn, was the filling station. There is still a plaque on the town hall wall in Exchange Street which says 'Corporation Gas Dept.' and a hand points to the words 'Gas containers for motor vehicles filled here'.

Thomas Burton, a native of Blackburn, had a workshop near his home in Cherry Tree, where he repaired penny farthing bicycles, and about the year 1900 he made his first motorcycle. Success stimulated his ambition and his next move was to construct a motor car which would be a great achievement. He built a three-horsepower motor tricycle which was used by the late Dr. Bannister in his practice for several years.

Mr Burton established a workshop in Park Road, Blackburn during the First World War and without doubt was recognised as the leading authority in the district on anything to do with motor car engineering.

Cars of that time were very unlike cars of today – they were apt to be more temperamental and more stubborn than any mule. On the earliest cars the rear driving chain would often break or jump off the sprocket wheel. In either case the chain was so well greased and dirty that any attempt to mend it covered your hands and clothes with the stuff. Motorists would venture far and wide through the country roads on these unreliable machines. Farmers 'reckoned nowt o' these new-fangled stinking contraptions', but did not hesitate to earn an honest bob by bringing horses to pull them to the top of the hill, or to drag them back onto the road out of a ditch.

There were no strict rules about parking and vehicles could be left anywhere as long as they were not causing an obstruction. Car doors were not locked, and when not in use the cars were hosed down, wiped off and kept in a shed. Nobody would think of leaving them at the kerb all night, or for longer periods.

Improvement of the roads to cope with the ever-increasing demands and pressures of heavy motor traffic was a major preoccupation of local authorities in the years after the First World War. Here, a Blackburn Corporation road gang, accompanied by a fine steamroller and an early cement mixer, are resurfacing and improving the road at Shear Brow in about 1920. Such fascinating activities always attracted a large gathering of schoolboys and by-standers, watching the work and captivated by the machines they used. To have a visiting photographer as well must have made the day of many a boy in the audience, while the workmen were by no means averse to pausing from their labours to pose with their shovels and machines.

A smartly-dressed signal lad chooses an unlikely perch for posing for a photographer at Spring Vale station in about 1910 – although the photographer must also be somewhere up a signal to obtain a fine high-level view. Spring Vale station was the next station south of Darwen on the line to Bolton. Opened by the grandly-named Bolton, Blackburn, Clitheroe and West Yorkshire Railway Company on the third of August 1847, it was the terminus of the line until Sough Tunnel could be opened on the second of June 1848, and the station itself was called Sough until 1870. In that year it became Spring Vale and Sough, and finally, in 1877, just Spring Vale. The railway company eventually reduced its title to a simple one – the Blackburn Railway, and in 1859, became part of the Lancashire and Yorkshire Railway system. Spring Vale station was closed on the fifth of August 1858, but there is now talk of re-opening it to passengers because of residential growth in south Darwen. This photograph illustrates well the forest of tall chimneys in the town – the India Mill chimney is especially prominent and seems to be a major contributor to the thick pall of smoke which hangs over Darwen, a pall which lasted a century.

By the 1880s in Blackburn several horse-bus routes had been established from various points in the town centre. These vehicles were primitive and uncomfortable, and matters were made worse by the shocking condition of the roads. But they were the first public conveyance which ordinary people might aspire to riding. By 1890 the Corporation had developed a horse-tram network with eight open-top, four-wheel, double-deck cars. Two animals were usually sufficient to haul one car, but three were needed for the steeper middle slopes of Preston New Road. Up to seventy horses were stabled in a building in Simmons Street, served by a branch line from Sudell Cross. The depot was used for the first electric cars, introduced when the system began to be electrified in 1899. There were also steam trams on the routes to Church and along Whalley New Road, while the Blackburn and Over Darwen Tramways Company ran steam trams on the route to Darwen.

Throughout its long service the Blackburn Corporation Tramways gave a valuable means of transport to the ordinary townspeople. There were increasing objections, of course. They were said to cause congestion because they could not move round other vehicles, a growing problem as the motor age developed. Passengers getting on and off trams in the middle of busy streets ran the risk of being knocked down by motor cars.

The trams could rattle along at a good rate, swaying about as though they would leave the rails. One alarming thing about them was the long seats which ran the full length of the tram – they were made of highly polished wood, and if the driver applied his brakes suddenly passengers were apt to slide along the seat and finish in a heap at the front end. Sometimes on market days the lorries loading or unloading at the fruit market, would completely block Victoria Street and trams trying to get through would be delayed for a long time, with the driver frantically – and often fruitlessly – stamping on his bell! It was said that trams with covered top decks were always sent on the 'posh' Preston New Road and Wilpshire routes, while the travellers on the other routes, riding on the open decks, were referred to as 'wet heads!'

Blackpool

O reminiscence of the 1910s and '20s could possibly be complete without some reference to Blackpool. Blackpool was 'the playground of Blackburn', the breezes off the sea were a tonic, the fresh air and ozone a health restorer. At home the hundreds of enormous mill chimneys and the open coal fires in their many thousands filled the atmosphere with a pall of smoke and grime that covered everything with soot. Soot in the milk on the doorstep; soot on the newly washed clothes hanging on the line, soot floating on the horses' drinking trough – no wonder people of all ages welcomed the few days on the coast, and in the sea, to get away from all the dirt and smoke of home, as well as to get away from the endless drudgery of everyday life for a well-earned rest.

The railways quickly became perfectly organised to carry hordes of people to the Lancashire coast. They looked forward all year to their holiday week, for which they had saved money all year round. When the time came, they packed everything they thought they would need, including food, into a tin trunk. The stations were thronged with people and there was a mad rush to get on the trains when they came in. By 1925 over four hundred trains a day(!) were arriving at Blackpool in the peak of the season, and on the August Bank Holiday of that year, the railways dealt with 473 special excursion trains to Blackpool, Fleetwood and Morecambe from all parts of the country.

During Wakes Week special boat trains carried people in their thousands to Liverpool, and in particular to Fleetwood, for steamers to the Isle of Man. The weekend midnight boat from Fleetwood was like a pleasure cruise gone mad. Trains were pulling into the station platforms and the people from each were hurriedly joining the queues on the quay and banging into each other with their luggage. Hundreds upon hundreds were lining the rails waving and shouting to their friends to 'hurry up'. The young people swarmed on board, and the ship was crowded to capacity. They kept their merriment up all night, singing, drinking and shuffling (no room to dance properly), they had a rare old 'rave up'. On the open decks they sang in bravado, 'I don't care if the ship goes down, for it doesn't belong to me.'

But above all else there was Blackpool. If you wanted to go, you were wise to book because if accommodation had not been booked in a boarding house well in advance, there would be nothing to be seen but 'No vacancies' signs in every window. Very few people stayed at home, and whole towns were quiet, almost like ghost towns.

Should you want a swim you went down to the sea and could make use of a bathing-machine drawn by a horse. The girls wore baggy things like boiler suits with frills around the ankles and cuffs. Groups of boys and girls, arm in arm, about twenty abreast, walked down the promenade carrying all before them, singing at the tops of their voices 'Yip I Addy I Aye I Aye' or 'Let's all go down the Strand and have a banana'. Lawrence Wright and Feldmann, the music publishers, thumped out the latest songs on their pianos, in open shops, and sold hundreds of Community Song Albums at sixpence each.

Cunningham's Holiday Homes, near the Derby Baths, were very popular. Boys stayed in one building or slept in tents, and the girls were locked, barred and bolted in another bulding! Ne'er the twain shall meet, after lights out, was the idea, but in the words of the old song, 'Love will find a way', and it did! Straw hats, lace-up boots and long skirts, a girl's face was her fortune, but with skirts down to her ankles her other resources could not be so easily estimated, and she firmly resisted any attempt to view them before a contract had been signed. Virginity was protected by a nine-inch hatpin!

There was usually one hit song which caught on, and was hummed, whistled or sung by everybody during that particular season. Would it have been 'Red Sails in the Sunset', 'Let the Rest of the World go by', or perhaps 'Let the great big world keep turning'. Swimming from bathing machines, chaps in long-legged one-piece costumes with vivid stripes, everybody paddling in the sea – salt water was 'good for the feet', so the women-folk tucked up their skirts into their baggy bloomers and ventured forth. Blackpool!

Into the country

EOPLE were so much restricted and directed in their daily lives, and had so little chance to escape, that when the opportunity came to get out of town and into the fresh air, they took to it in their thousands. The call of the great outdoors, made possible by trains and bicycles and, later, charabancs, gave relaxation and exercise from walking, rambling gently or just sitting and looking at the scenery. On fine evenings, especially in the summer, people would wander down country lanes fragrant with honeysuckle, wild roses, mayflowers and new-mown hay. They would think nothing of a twenty-mile ride on their bikes before lighting-up time came . . . but sometimes you might be stopped by a policeman. He would ask you where you were going and, if you didn't have a lamp on your bike and he thought you couldn't reach your destination before lighting-up time, he could have turned you back.

An enjoyable day out at Easter, or at Whitsuntide, was to go by train to Clitheroe, stroll in the castle grounds or take a leisurely walk to Brungerley Bridge to spend an afternoon boating on the river. There might be outings in horse-drawn wagonettes, a very enjoyable feature of the holiday season – not forgetting, though, that in the hilly areas passengers were sometimes asked to get off and walk! They were even expected to get out and *push* to help the horses on the very steep hills. Nevertheless, driving through quiet country lanes and villages, eating strawberries and cream in a secluded tea-garden was 'Paradise Enow,

Off for a day out in their splendid eighteen-seater, open-top charabanc (speed limit twelve miles per hour) are these Blackburners of the early 1920s. Their destination is unknown, and neither do we know who the group is. A club or society or church outing, perhaps? It was in vehicles such as this that, for the first time, people from the towns could go off en masse *into remote countryside and quiet villages (quiet until the charas came . . .), enjoying the scenery and anticipating the bargain tea and a drink at the end of the outing.*

with thou beside me'.

Rambling became very popular in the 1930s. Hordes of young people with rucksacks and hob-nailed boots strode out o'er moor and fell, from Pendle Hill to Waddington Fell and the Wiswell Moors, sampling, perhaps, the 'Barley Water' on the way? But earlier, we had rambled too. A favourite outing was from Wilpshire via Salesbury Church and Copster Green, passing 'Lovely Hall' on your right, then through a farmyard and over the fields to the De Tabley at Ribchester. Here you kept to the right bank of the river to Sale Wheel Woods and Dinckley Ferry. Here you shouted as loud as you could until a little old man appeared on the other bank and rowed a small boat across to you. On one occasion four small boys wanted to go across, but as the charge was a penny each, and four pennies was a lot of money, three of the boys unashamedly stripped off and swam over. The other boy picked up their clothes and went across on the boat for one penny. The boatman perhaps, only pretended to be angry! From the ferry you went up the hill to Hurst Green, passing the Shireburn Arms on the right. There, in a small, clean cottage, a frail old lady dressed in black with a white apron, would make you a meal of a boiled egg, stewed rhubarb, bread and butter and a cup of tea, which for two people would cost altogether sixpence (two and a half new pence) – that was in 1918.

Tramping on again to Lower Hodder Bridge, where Oliver Cromwell and his armies had paused in 1648 on the evening before the Battle of Preston, you passed close by Stonyhurst. In the 1930s we tuned in on our wireless sets to Father Rowland of the College Observatory, who gave a very reliable weather forecast after the 8 a.m. news bulletin. Leaving all this behind you walked the few uneventful miles to Whalley to catch the train, crowded with hikers who had spent the day at Settle or Ingleton and were returning to Blackburn, Bolton or Manchester. And so home, to Wilpshire and Blackburn, tired after a long but thoroughly enjoyable day.

If you wanted to give your legs a vigorous stretching, you could venture into witch country at Worston or Barley. The only witches seen on frequent rambles over and around Pendle were blue-eyed maidens who held you in their spell from which you could not easily escape – even if you tried, which you did not always want to do. On Pendle, near to Roughlea, was Malkin Tower, the supposed meeting-place of the Devil and his witches. Wild tales were told of orgies and other goings-on at the dead of night at Malkin Tower. If you tried hard enough you could imagine the ghostly shapes in the gloom of a foggy day, and think uncomfortably about all the old stories.

In 1937, feeling in need of a holiday of a very different sort, I sailed to Norway in the British India line ship, *City of Nagpur*. It was a six-day cruise to Christiansand and Oslo, and the all-in fare was just six pounds. In 1938 I went on the *Dilwara* to Copenhagen. This was a nine-day cruise, and a lot more expensive – twelve pounds. It was in Copenhagen that a party of us from the ship were chased by the guard for singing outside the king's palace . . . at three o'clock in the morning.

Entertainment

I remember I had been taken by my father one Easter Fair morning to see the first moving picture show that came to Blackburn. It was just a converted magic lantern standing on an orange box, the light flickering as the frames were passing through the box. Much later I was to see the first 'talkie' to come to the town, with Al Jolson singing 'Mammy'.

At home we had an Edison Bell gramophone, with wax cylinder records and a great big horn hanging from the ceiling. Among the tunes I remember best were 'The Miner's Dream of Home', 'When The Fields Are White With Daisies' and, believe it or not, 'Give Me A Ticket To Heaven Before The Last Train Has Gone'.

Outside in the street, there might be German bands and catchy-poley bears. A German band would suddenly appear in your street and play a few tunes, collect a few coppers and then go away again. Some people gave them an odd copper – a penny – and told them to go away and play in the next street. Sometimes a foreign-looking man – he could, perhaps, have been from one of the Balkan states – wearing tough, hard-wearing clothes and with a feather in his hat, would pull a reluctant bear into your street. The bear was muzzled and had a metal ring through its nose with a rope attached to it. After a few fierce tugs on the rope the bear was in so much pain that it was induced to give a little dance without any music. The bear stood upright and caught the pole which the keeper threw to it and then it cocked over its tail. There were no little children on the street, they were all peeping safely from behind the curtains in their homes, but bigger boys enjoyed performing as the bear; they pulled a potato sack over their heads with

The Albert Hall Cinema Orchestra, Darwen, in about 1926. There are not many photographs of cinema orchestras, once such an essential attribute of all cinemas of quality before sound took over in the early-1930s. The orchestra had a difficult task – warming up, filling in, accompanying the film with appropriate sounds, and finally giving a good send off to the departing audience. Here we have the pride of the Albert Hall, Darwen. Left to right: Tom Field, ?, Stanley Garland, ? The Manager, Corrie Briggs, Bob (Jock) Cooper, Harry Martin.

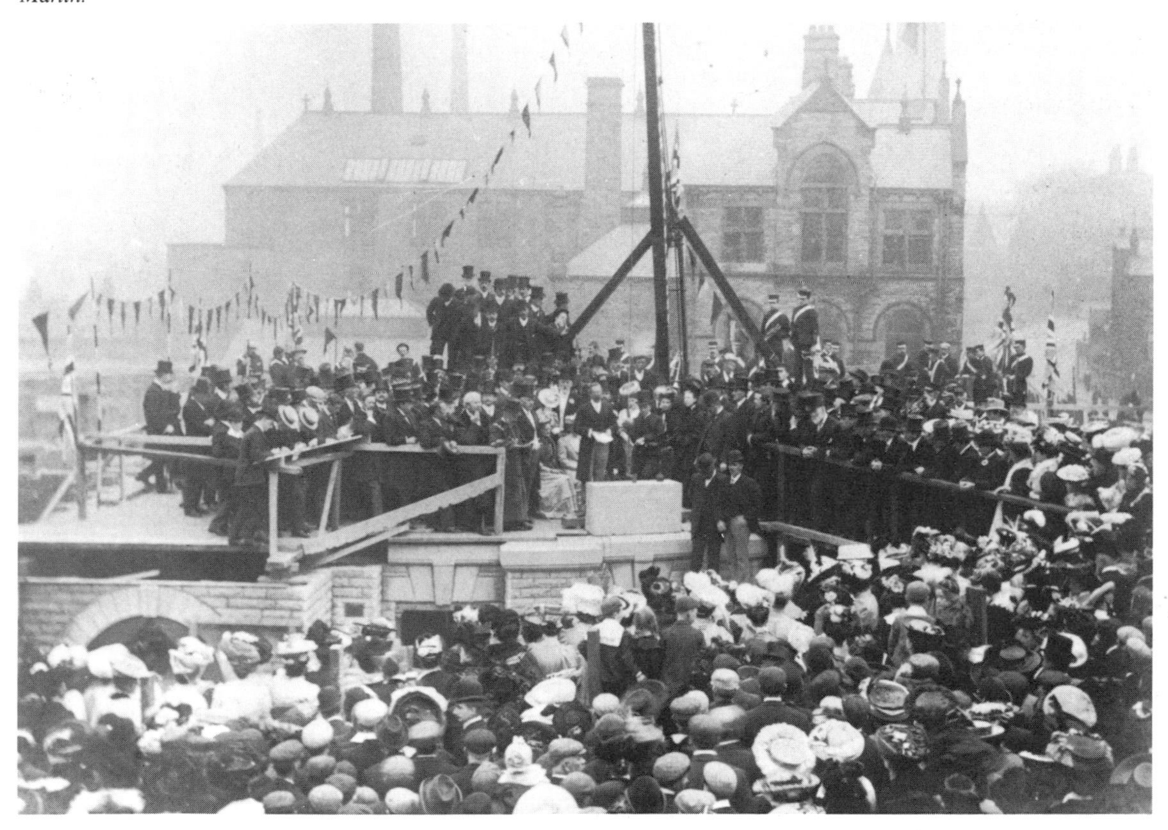

Public libraries were one of the main means of 'self-improvement' available to ordinary people, and many were established in the nineteenth century by local authorities or charitable bodies, or, in the late years of the century and up to the 1914-18 War, by the Carnegie Trust, set up by Andrew Carnegie, the Scottish-born multi-millionaire, American philanthropist and industrialist. The library at Darwen was a Carnegie endowment, and the foundation stone of the impressive building on its prominent corner site was laid at a well-attended ceremony in 1904, although, as can be seen, the work on the building was already in progress. The library was opened in 1908 by no less a personage than Andrew Carnegie himself.

Corporation Park was one of the greatest public parks in mid-Victorian Britain. It began with a fifty-five acre site purchased by the new Corporation of Blackburn in the early-1850s, and was opened, in the presence of 60,000 people, in 1857. Hundreds of unemployed millworkers were engaged in public relief works there during the great cotton famine in the 1860s, and there were later extensions and improvements. The opening of the park was marked by a public holiday in the town, and two Russian cannons captured in the Crimean War, were placed in the park. The new park gave a desperately-needed breathing space, a 'lung' of fresh air open to the people of Blackburn, and with its fine views across the valley and town, forested with smoking chimneys, it was a major local attraction. There were few more popular places for a Sunday afternoon walk, dressed in your best Sunday clothes, chatting to friends and neighbours passed on the way. The children could enjoy the lake and – small boys especially – the two great cannon, which were unfortunately melted down in another conflict, the Second World War.

Darwen was a much smaller town than Blackburn, and beautiful countryside, open moorland and attractive streams and valleys were within easy reach on all sides. It was not difficult to walk for ten or fifteen minutes and be out of the smoke and noise of the town. Even the River Darwen, polluted as it was by the thirty-nine mills, ten paper mills and thousands of houses of the town, retained traces of its rural past. This view, dated about 1910, shows the river below Hollins Grove, approximately where the sewage works is today.

Blackburn Rovers Football Club was founded in 1875, and very quickly became an outstanding team and one of the pioneers of professional football in Britain. It also, very quickly, became the object of passionate pride in the hearts of all true Blackburners, and its early triumphs brought onto the streets crowds of the size more associated with returning heroes of our own day. The team shown here is that of 1881-1882, well on their way to the triumphant years 1884 to 1895, when winning the Cup and supplying England internationals seemed to be a speciality unique to Blackburn Rovers!

slits in the sides for their arms, and tied a rope around their waist. They could catch a pole and topple over their tails, and their black sooty faces readily brought pennies from passers-by.

These goings-on usually took place in May time, when the little girls in their prettiest frocks danced around the maypole on the green, in the streets, or on the market ground. They danced around the Queen, who was holding the maypole, and they sang:

Round and round the maypole merrily we go
tripping, tripping lightly, singing as we go
All the happy pastimes on the village green,
Sporting in the sunshine, hurrah for the Queen.

The Queen, standing, then sang:

I'm the queen, don't you see,
Just come from the meadow green,
and if you will wait for a little while,
I will dance you the maypole style.
My hair is long, my dress is short,
My boots are laced with silver,
A red rosette upon my breast,
And a guinea gold ring on my finger.

A lady remembers one of the happy May Day celebrations in which she took part; the year was about 1920. In the village of Tockholes, where she lived, everything was hurry and bustle. The farmers brought their horses, the milkman his horse and cart, some children brought their ponies. The horses' coats, hooves, and brasses were polished to shine and manes and tails were plaited and woven into intricate patterns with flowers and coloured ribbons.

'My hair was a shade of auburn,' she said, 'long and wavy. I wore a hairband of gilt and diamante, my lovely dress, white socks and black velvet dancing pumps.'

There was a general stir as we got into our places for the procession. Two brewery shire horses led the way (proudly beautiful), and the other horses followed. Next came our 'May Queen'. To a march played by a silver band we paraded round the village streets to Farmer Turner's field where the maypole was in position. Events followed events, the Queen did the tour of honour round the fields to much

Blackburn Public Library in 1926. The first picture shows the Reference Library (with prominently displayed large notice, 'Silence is requested'), while the second shows the Children's Library, the extraordinary sight of every child very studiously and intently looking into a large open volume would suggest that this picture was carefully arranged well in advance, to give the right impression!

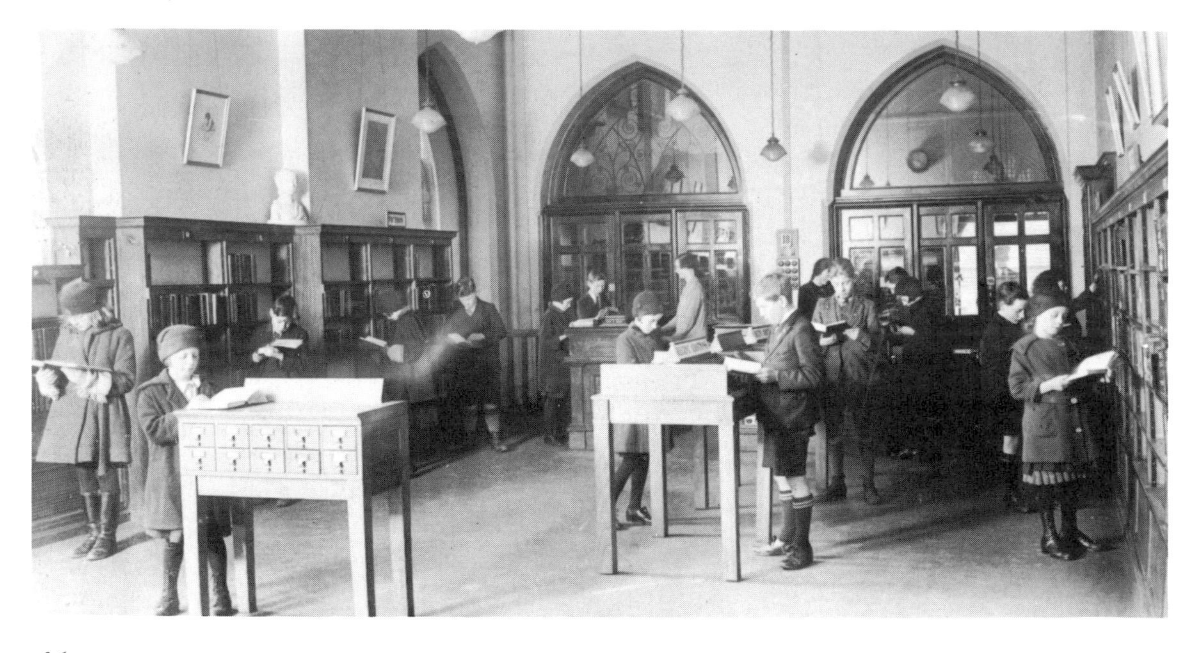

enthusiastic and appreciative clapping and cheering. The beautiful horses paraded and were awarded prizes of rosettes according to merit. There was a sack race, egg and spoon race, judging of the children's pets and a Punch and Judy show and we were each given a glass of dandelion and burdock.

And now it was time for the last event of the day, 'The Grande Finale'. We took our places, she recalled, the ribbons were untied, and we each took one – and then we were away – in and out, out and in, over and under, under and over, round and round and round until at last there was the maypole with coloured ribbons attached at one end to the top, and at the other clenched in the sweaty hands of a troupe of little girls in their pretty best dresses. The applause was tremendous, clapping, cheering, hurrahs, and a lot of laughing, we had to curtsy and curtsy again and again. Then we sat down to sandwiches, pies, savoury rolls, cakes, jellies and trifles.

And after that, tired and yawing, it was over. Our lovely day.

If you were so minded you could read, with the help of the Public Library. In the Blackburn Public Lending Library there were no books on display or shelves for you to browse along. A medium-height desk ran the full length of the room and on it were bulky catalogues of all the books in the library. You looked in the catalogues for your favourite authors and wrote on a card the classification and number of the books you wished to borrow. You then handed it to an attendant, who disappeared and then returned with the books if they were available. To be successful at this game you had to have some knowledge of literature and authors in the first place – no good taking a chance! Books by authors such as Marie Corelli, Wilkie Collins and Charles Reade, *The Cloister and the Hearth,* were popular, as were the more serious authors – Dickens, Stevenson, the Brontes and Kipling. Daring readers chose Oscar Wilde, while those who wanted excitement

Blakey Moor, the open triangle of waste ground behind Northgate, was long ago a piece of grazing moor as its name suggests. It then became the market and fairground, and was one of the few open spaces in the centre of the old town where people might perambulate. Such an activity was generally associated with the very poor who could not afford more expensive or sophisticated amusements, so a wander on a summer day was their only choice. This very early picture shows Blakey Moor from the corner of Nab Lane, in 1887. Most people are simply standing and talking, or strolling around in small groups, a welcome break from the grind and drudgery of daily life.

For the poorer working man there was often nowhere to meet or congregate after work, apart from the beer houses, until the working men's clubs became widespread in the second half of the nineteenth century. The club at Hoddlesden was founded in 1868, and this photograph was taken in about 1880. It shows the members of the club in the company, for reasons unknown, of a uniformed constable – a working man himself, of course. The picture is of interest for the array of different types of working clothes and outfits which it depicts.

could get hold of Conan Doyle's works. If you read a lot, though, you were called a bookworm, and if you were considered to be well-read, you were being paid a great compliment, by some people at least.

There was usually at least one member of the family who played a musical instrument. Somebody could be expected to play a piano, a concertina, a violin or even a mouth organ. On Sunday nights there might be a great get-together of all the family to have a really good sing-song. Children would play at Ludo, Snakes and Ladders, Hide the Thimble or Blind Man's Buff, joining in every now and again to sing the hymns they knew or particularly liked. On Saturday nights, apart from going to the 'pictures', the Sunday School social might be tempting. They had concerts, games and dancing, usually in the school hall, but unfortunately very few clergymen approved of dancing.

Drinking was rife in the towns; beer was only five pence (two new pence) a pint, or forty-eight pints for one pound - but bear in mind that one pound was more than half of a week's wage. Perhaps because of this, or just because it was good entertainment, Mrs Lewis drew lots of people to her Temperance Mission in Mincing Lane in Blackburn. She had a head of white curls which fell to her shoulders, and during the singing of a hymn she would call out, inviting the audience to 'Come and be saved'. Many people would kneel at the front of the stage, but all sorts of people, gifted or otherwise, would climb onto the platform to 'do a turn'. Notices on the walls stated that 'Lips that touch liquor shall never touch mine', 'Yield not to temptation' and 'Dare to be a Daniel and sign the pledge'.

Besides making your own enjoyment there were a few versatile people who joined amateur orchestras and concert groups, or the forerunners of the now widespread amateur dramatic societies. In Darwen there were several very talented entertainers, among them Tommy Cherry, remembered for his troupe of negro minstrels, and John Reed on the piano. They deserve to be recalled for the pleasure they brought to the people of the town in the depressed days of the 1930s. They wrote 'The Darren Mashers', a skit on the residents of Back Duckworth Street. It was always well received, and it became their 'signature tune':

'We are the two Darren Mashers,
We often go out on the Mash.
We wear no tall hats, or no shirts
To our backs,
And seldom we have any cash.
We oftimes bring out the new fashion
And seldom stick to the old,
Although we are just twenty-seven
We're handsome, stout-hearted and bold.

So we sing Tra-la-la!
As we walk down the street
We're the two Darren Mashers from
Back Duckworth Street'.

There were two outstanding entertainers with John Reed – Mary Marsh and her sister Kathleen. From 1937 onwards they appeared as the 'Melodettes' and raised a lot of money for charities, becoming well-known and popular in all the east Lancashire towns.

There had been a Blackburn Amateur Theatrical Company as long ago as 1837, but it was not until 1912 that the new Blackburn Amateur

Daily routines, then as now, were punctuated by exciting events, but life before the advent of shorter working weeks, longer holidays, greater financial security, mass entertainment and leisure and easy transport, was often a great deal more routine and more difficult, and the exciting events seemed all the more exciting. But some events, such as special royal occasions, produce the same enthusiasm now as they did eighty years ago. Here is Darwen market place gaily decorated in 1912 for the celebrations to mark the coronation of their Majesties, King George V and Queen Mary. Crowds gather, there is festivity in the air, and the schoolchildren play their part – but how difficult it must have been to get those frocks so white in the sooty atmosphere of Darwen!

Dramatic and Musical Society came into being, and became a favourite with the townspeople. Their first performance was given in Anvil Street New Church School on the tenth of October 1912, but the society's first major production was a one night performance in the Olympia Theatre in April 1913, a performance widely regarded as 'magnificent' and one which played to a packed house. In December 1913 they gave Bernard Shaw's 'You Never Can Tell' at the same venue, and in 1916 their performance of 'The New Boy' was so successful that they were asked to repeat it at the Military Hospital at Whalley.

The 'Blackburn Amateurs', as they were generally known, were a remarkably talented lot. They made their own scenery and costumes and the orchestra was made up entirely of local musicians. Their repertoire of musical comedy set a very high standard and productions were looked forward to with keen anticipation, as they were regarded as one of the leading social events of the season. My first introduction to a musical comedy by them was in the Theatre Royal to see 'The Quaker Girl'. The young lady's boss had given her two tickets, which opened up an exciting impression of plush and gold, the orchestra tuning up on their plaintive instruments and the air heavy with perfume and cigar smoke.

High days and holidays

HE biggest annual event in Blackburn, by far, was the Easter Fair which was held on the market ground. There were all kinds of roundabouts and amusements for adults and children in profusion. There was the helter-skelter and the cake-walk, hobby horses and motor cars, side shows with the 'fat lady' and the 'Flea Circus', a boxing booth open to all-comers to challenge the champ (a purse for the winner). All the mechanical amusements were driven by the enormous power generated by the great steam traction engines. These engines, beautiful to look at, were so heavy that as they rumbled along the streets at about four miles an hour they almost shook the houses down! The organs on the roundabouts all seemed to be playing different tunes, adding to the overall effect of indescribable noise.

A chair on a lorry carried a notice: 'Teeth painlessly extracted, consultations free'. Professor Yankee Doodle claimed to be from Boston, U.S.A., and accompanying him on the lorry were two musicians, one playing a drum and the other a trombone. Altogether there was so much noise that you couldn't tell if the operation was painless or not!

At the same time the annual Pot Fair was held on the market ground, opposite what is now Marks and Spencers store. This was a very popular event and people flocked in from neighbouring districts to replenish their crockery. One of the principal attractions, though,

And in the following year, 1913, even more excitement. The King and Queen came to Lancashire and visited both Blackburn and Darwen, drawing huge, cheering crowds to the centres of both towns and along their route in between. The first picture shows Lord Derby, the Lord Lieutenant of Lancashire, presenting John Duckworth to Queen Mary at Blackburn Town Hall on the tenth of July 1913. The second view is of the grand and elaborately-decorated wooden platform erected to receive the royal party outside Darwen Town Hall. The King and Queen are about to leave and are making their farewells to the civic dignitaries of the town and its industries. The King may be seen talking to the Mayor just to the right of the left hand column. The Queen is on the King's left with the Mayoress, who quite eclipses the Queen by her magnificent feather boa and hat!

was not what was on sale, but the skilled salesmanship of the auctioneers themselves. One such man was Mr Dalyell. Crockery, safely packed in straw and housed in very large crates would be delivered by the railway horse and lorry to his temporary stall on the market ground. Mr Dalyell's men would set out and prepare the stage for the entry of this immaculately dressed showman. The diamonds on his fingers and his tie-pin would sparkle in the light from dozens of electric light bulbs, and his supreme artistry raised the baskets of pots to nothing less than works of art, which he was condescending to sell to the people of Blackburn as a special favour.

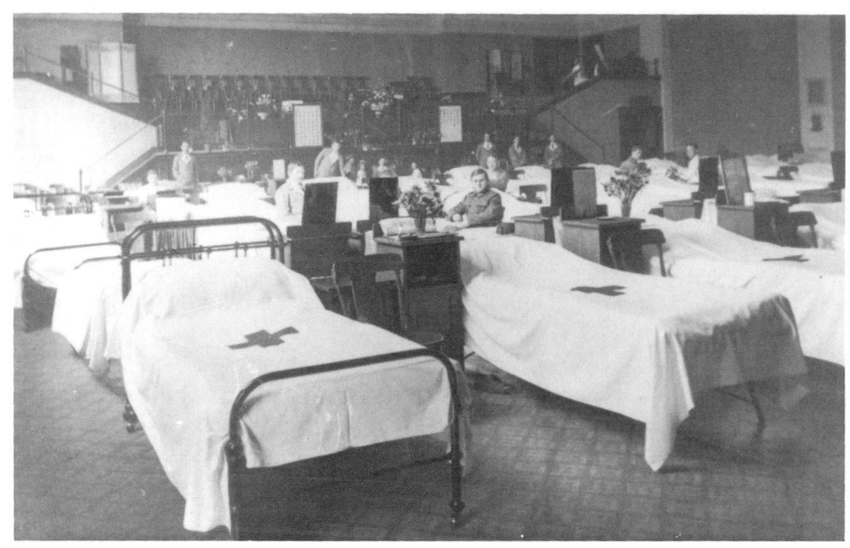

During the 1914-18 War thousands of Blackburn and Darwen men volunteered or were called up and hundreds lost their lives. At home suitable (and occasionally unsuitable) buildings might be requisitioned for service as wartime military hospitals for the less badly wounded and the vast numbers of convalescent soldiers. They were staffed by volunteer nurses and orderlies to assist the hard-pressed regular personnel. Local people provided comforts for the troops – books, flowers, cigarettes, food, company and conversation – and many such hospitals were 'adopted' by the community. This view shows the Blackburn Public Halls, converted for use as a military hospital in 1916.

On Saturday the twenty-sixth of September 1931 a particularly exotic dignitary visited Darwen – although he would not have regarded himself as a dignitary, rather the opposite. Mahatma Ghandi came to the town with an Indian delegation, looking at the cotton industry (Darwen had traditionally close links with the Indian cotton trade,, as the name India Mills indicates). Ghandi wore his customary robe and sandals, and looks distinctly incongruous among the soberly-clad representatives of town and industry who accompanied the delegation on its visit.

Easter was a special time in any case, the time of 'coming to life' of lambs and chickens, daffodils and buds on the trees. The end of winter was marked by the 'spoiling' of the children – they enjoyed themselves at the fair, were given new clothes and perhaps new toys bought in the market hall. The old custom of pace-egging was almost extinct in Blackburn by the early-1880s, when John Harland wrote *Lancashire Folk Lore,* and by the early years of this century it was recalled only by the children running from shop to shop shouting 'Pace egg please' and being given ginger biscuits by harassed shopkeepers in an attempt to pacify them!

Shrove Tuesday, commonly called Pancake Tuesday, was traditionally spent in merry-making and in gorging with food to make up for the abstinence which would be required during the following weeks of Lent. Most people looked forward to having pancakes on that day, and of course it was a special treat for the kiddies. It was good fun watching the pancakes being tossed up (sometimes they hit the ceiling), but more often than not they dropped back into the pan, bottom-side up. Everybody enjoyed Shrove Tuesday. It was customary for the apprentices to finish work at noon on that day, but they had to watch out because if their workmates caught them there would be a great deal of horseplay, and they would have to go home with their faces blackened.

The Thursday before Whitsuntide was commemorated in many Lancashire towns (and especially in Manchester and Salford) by the holding of huge processions. Dressed appropriately in white, and holding huge banners, the people, mostly children, walked through the

At the end of the Great War there was a brief economic boom, followed by a dramatic collapse in 1920. The Lancashire textile industries suffered badly from the loss of their traditional markets, which had been cut off during the war, and as a result there was serious unemployment, wage-cutting and unrest in the industry. This photograph shows a scene during the 1920-21 millworkers' strike. It was taken in the Nab Lane area of Blackburn, and shows striking mill-girls guarded, or restrained, by a large contingent of the Blackburn Borough Police Force.

The war dead were commemorated and remembered for all time in every community throughout the land by the erection and dedication of war memorials in the early-1920s. The unveiling ceremonies were the occasions for massive public remembrance of the dead, for scarcely anyone had not lost a relative or a friend. In this picture we see the service of the unveiling of the Darwen War Memorial on the twenty-fourth of September 1921.

Darwen was given a charter of incorporation as a borough in 1978. It had had a Local Board of Health since 1853, but its rise in population and commercial importance meant that borough status could be justified. The new borough acquired the full complement of civic regalia, civic officials and civic occasions. The mayor-making ceremony, instituted in 1879, quickly became a traditional event and, as in other towns, involved a procession through the town of the new mayor, the Corporation and its officers, the clergy and other leading figures in the life of Darwen. This view shows the procession which took place in 1936.

streets, and if you were travelling by road you would find sections of the main roads closed to traffic for several hours at a time. And then, best of all, there was Christmas.

Weeks of saving – weeks of preparation – another little one to bless us this Christmas – time for children to shout up the chimney – 'It would take a horse and cart to fetch that lot' – noses pressed against shop windows – 'Join our Christmas club' – pay two pence or even sixpence a week for twelve weeks – Christmas tree bright with candles – holly and mistletoe hanging high.

Aunts, uncles, cousins, stamping snow off their boots – 'Come in, come, in, give me your coat' – hugs and kisses – more presents – iced cakes, mince pies – chicken and trifle – too full for words – 'Hush, little carol singers, wet and blue with cold – make room by the fire' – hot milk – more mince pies – presents off the tree – a few pennies – oranges clutched in tiny fingers.

Spirit of Christmas – share what you have with others – John's old coat – David's shoes (they're too small for him now) – goodbye, goodbye – run home quickly.

A sudden blizzard – auntie from 'out back' in the candlelight – 'too bad to walk all the way home now' – Hurrah! six little heads in a bed – three at the top, three at the bottom.

Silent night, holy night
All is calm, all is bright
Round yon Virgin Mother and child
Holy infant so tender and mild
Sleep in heavenly peace
Sleep in heavenly peace.

Around town

EFORE there were any bus shelters on Blackburn Boulevard there was just a small white tiled building, isolated in the middle of the great area of open road. This was the cabbies' shelter, where in bad weather they kept warm and dry inside the hut and the horses waited outside, steaming and taking a well-earned rest.

Work on laying out the Boulevard as a proper open space with shelters and roadways began in 1881, but it was a slow process. Queen Victoria began her vigil there in 1905. But apart from the railway passengers it remained a fairly quiet place. When the trains came in the newspaper boys shouted their special editions, while the 'hot potato men' stood by their trucks and carts, hoping for custom. But gradually, the Boulevard became busier and busier, when at first the trams and later the buses used it for a terminus.

In 1914 and 1915 the famous recruiting poster 'Your King and Country Need YOU' drew more and more volunteers, and the Boulevard was the scene of their gathering. Hundreds and hundreds of them marched there and paraded before the station, four abreast through the booking hall and onto their platform, destined, all too soon in retrospect, for 'the front'.

Gladstone had joined Queen Victoria on the Boulevard, but as in real life, she must have grown tired of his company – perhaps she was 'not amused' – for later his monument was moved to a position in front of the Technical College.

Surely the most spectacular event ever to have been witnessed by the Boulevard was the triumphal homecoming of the Blackburn Rovers in 1884, an event recorded in detail by Charles Francis in his *History of the Blackburn Rovers Football Club* published to commemorate their fiftieth anniversary in 1925.

> When the all conquering Rovers brought the Association Cup home in March 1844 the enthusiasm of the inhabitants knew no bounds. The square in front of the railway was packed with a cheering multitude and the streets were almost impassable owing to the dense throngs who had assembled to welcome the heroes of the occasion.

Flooding was a recurrent problem in nineteenth- and early-twentieth-century Blackburn and Darwen, and it still occurs occasionally. The building of houses, streets and mills not just alongside the rivers but actually on top of them was a partial cause of the problem. The flood prevention works were minimal and the drainage networks just could not cope with a heavy Pennine cloudburst. The first picture shows Duckworth Street, Darwen, during the floods of the eighteenth of June 1905 (not too deep, as the pavement and the tramtracks are still visible). The second shows the much more serious flooding of central Blackburn in February 1907, when the waters were six feet deep in some places. This scene is at Salford Bridge.

Before and after. The Darwen Corporation built new swimming baths in the early-1930s to replace those which had been used since the 1850s. The 'before' picture shows the derelict properties on the site of the baths in 1924, before their clearance and demolition. The 'after' picture shows the imposing new baths, which were finished in 1932 and officially opened the following year by H.R.H. Prince George, Duke of Kent. The provision of public baths was originally intended primarily for the purposes of cleanliness, not of leisure (there was no leisure!), and many were accompanied by public wash-houses and laundries. But by the 1930s the idea of swimming baths as a place for healthy swimming as a pleasure, not a necessity, was widespread.

This was the culmination of a magnificent few years for the Blackburn team, including some astonishing feats of goal-scoring, with Rovers often achieving figures well into the teens!

> An imposing procession, containing seven large equipages, was led by the Borough Brass Band, behind whom rode the victorious team in a gaily beflagged wagonette drawn by six spanking greys. Next came the Committee and Members of the Press who were followed by representatives of the Olympic (late holders of the trophy) in a big

conveyance decorated with flags and drawn by eight horses with three postilions in red jackets and velvet caps. The Livesey Band, in uniform, brought up the rear.

Horses were a universally common sight in the town, and until the First World War motor vehicles were still a rarity. The roads, and especially the main roads, were filthy, and often ankle-deep in horse manure. The long skirts of the women trailed in the dust and the mud and in everything else which fouled the pavements. In summer, the dirt and the manure attracted great swarms of flies which invaded the house and covered everything indoors. Sticky flycatchers could be seen in every house, shop and office, but there still seemed to be more flies than ever.

The noise and the dirt and the smell of the town were often appalling – though in different ways the town is as noisy and dirty and

Fire Brigades, formed by volunteers and paid for by public subscription or by the local authority, existed in many communities, although contemporary accounts suggest that many were not too effective when it came to real fires! During the nineteenth century many borough and town councils took over the management of fire brigades, and provided better equipment and training, but it was often still volunteers who manned the brigade. Darwen's first volunteer brigade was formed in 1836, and its first engine, a manually-operated horse-drawn cart, is shown here. The other picture shows one of the horse-drawn steam fire-engines of the Blackburn brigade outside the Clayton Street fire station in 1905. The impressive array of highly-polished brassware, both on the engine itself and on the helmets and uniforms of the men, is typical of the pride felt in the brigade by its members, and by the people of the town. The Clayton street fire station was closed in December 1921 and replaced by the new station in Canterbury Street.

King William Street and Blackburn Town Hall, about 1900. On the right can be seen the end of the outdoor market, while the decorative and very ornamental standards supporting the overhead wires for the newly-electrified tramway system are also much in evidence. The arrival of a photographer was, as always, 'an event', and the usual complement of small and not-so-small boys has also been captured for posterity. The Town Hall, 'an edifice in the Italian style', was built at a cost of over £30,000 in 1856.

Boulevard in about 1895, showing (on the right) a steam tram and a four-wheeled cab. The Boulevard at this time was already being used as a terminus for public transport, outside the railway station, but it had not yet become the hub of numerous bus and tram services which it was in the 1920s and 1930s. Its openness was as yet uncluttered by all the shelters and notices of a bus terminus, and so the fine examples of Blackburn's excellent Victorian Gothic architecture at the town end could be readily appreciated.

Church Street, Blackburn, in 1898. The freedom from traffic is perhaps the most striking feature of this view. Church Street was one of the main town centre streets, but although it was photographed on a reasonably busy shopping day it was possible for all those who were fascinated by the photographer and his camera to stand, completely at ease and free from danger, in the middle of the road. The scene has changed quite dramatically since then as swirling traffic, direction signs, traffic lights and a giant shopping precinct have transformed the peaceful scene.

smelly now. But with no bathroom at home and no easy means of washing clothes it was often very difficult for our forebears to keep clean even if they wanted to. For that reason many towns established public baths and wash-houses, to which people could go if the facilities at home were inadequate or non-existent. In Darwen, the Baths and Wash-house Committee was set up in 1853, a pioneering effort on the part of a number of people who collected subscriptions for its erection. There was no town council in Darwen at that date, neither was there any drainage or sewerage system, and little real idea of sanitation, so the provision of the old baths was a notable achievement on the part of the townspeople. These baths, the Peel Baths, were very small, and by the turn of the century the building had become quite badly dilapidated. For many years it had been even more cramped as the baths building also housed the offices of the town clerk, the rate collector, the borough surveyor and the school attendance officer(!), and these only moved in 1882 when the new market hall and municipal buildings were opened.

One of the best things that Darwen Corporation ever did was to build the new swimming baths which were opened by the Duke of Kent, Prince George, in 1933. In the new baths building, the idea of mixed bathing was viewed with some suspicion, even in the 1940s. It was only accepted gradually (it had been decreed that there was to be no 'messing about!'). The breakdown of the barriers began with letting the ladies have some time in the baths to themselves during the week. After a while both sexes were allowed to be in the baths at the same time, but the men had to use the cabins on the left of the baths and the

The centre of Darwen was, until the 1880s, small and old-fashioned, with the old buildings of what was only fifty years before a village. The 1880s saw the large-scale redevelopment of the centre, with new public buildings, shops and offices, and the sweeping away of the more obvious traces of the eighteenth-century rural past. The Corporation, with its new market house and municipal buildings, set an example in this direction. This view, taken in 1880, shows Green Street and Market Street, with the Angel Inn *occupying the angle site between. The air of a Pennine hill village is still apparent in the quaint streets and traditional architecture and building materials.*

Another altered scene. Sudell Cross, taken from King William Street in 1906. The tram tracks and overhead standards on Preston New Road and Limbrick are the signs of the modern age – they were then only seven years old – but a single horse-drawn delivery cart is the only vehicle in sight . . . though to judge by the deposits on the road surface, other horses had passed this way not long before!

In the early-1890s a large site was cleared of its old buildings to make way for Millstone, a splendid and imposing part of the new town centre. The view shows the demolition work in progress.

ladies the cabins on the other side. In the water the same rule applied, and if anyone strayed to the 'wrong' side an attendant blew a whistle and told them to go back. But it wasn't long before there was more freedom of movement; it was a good opportunity, so the bathers said, to teach each other to swim . . .

A survey of Darwen carried out in 1931 showed that the principal industries of the town were paper-making and cotton. There were, it reported, thirty-nine cotton mills and ten paper mills (as well as twenty-eight 'hotels!'). On the face of it this was a solid base for a prosperous town, but already the effects of the general depression were being felt. The cotton industry, in particular, was facing very severe competition from abroad, a problem which had started during the First World War. The Lancashire textile machinery had been copied in other countries, often from examples sold abroad by Lancashire firms, and students from countries which would be our rivals in the trade had been taught the principles of cotton manufacture in our

The rebuilding of the centre of Darwen was largely complete by 1900, and the old buildings had been replaced by larger and more impressive blocks in the latest architectural styles. This view of The Circus dates from about 1910, and gives a good impression of the change in character, if compared with the picture of the Angel Inn. *During the 1920s and 30s there was another bout of rebuilding, and in the 1970s several re-development schemes were carried out, not all of them commendable. The old Victorian and Edwardian town centre, itself only a century old, has thus been drastically altered and changed. How long will the supermarkets and concrete blocks of the 1960s and 1970s survive?*

technical colleges, notably those at Blackburn and Bolton. During the war the Japanese had taken over our markets in Japan itself, in China and in India, while both the Indians and the Chinese were developing their own flourishing trades in cotton. Our cotton men were getting badly into debt, and many firms were forced to close down. In 1928 for example, one of the pioneers of the trade, Formby's of Blackburn, tried to sell by public auction their weaving sheds and mills. There was none in all Lancashire who would do them the honour of even making a bid. Signs of the times to come.

Eventually, the mill chimneys that had belched smoke and filth, but which had meant a livelihood to thousands of families, were demolished. The tramway standards and the overhead cables disappeared, too, as the old tram systems in Blackburn and Darwen closed and made way for the motor bus. The ironworks chimney at Goosehouse Bridge also went in the 1930s. With the clearing of the chimneys and the end of their smoke and grime, the atmosphere cleared and the Jubilee Tower again became visible from Darwen. It used to be said that:

'If you can see the tower it's going to rain; if you can't see it, it's raining!'

A much earlier rhyme, very unjustly referring to the pollution from the industries of Darwen, went:

'Between two hills, both bleak and barren, lies dirty little Darren'.

Farewell to Blackburn

VEN before the First World War there had been those who found that the prospect of life in another country, and the opportunities which places like America and Australia offered, meant that life at home seemed harder to bear, with its grim conditions, low wages and – increasingly – the threat of problems in the staple industries of East Lancashire. The author's Aunt Grace and Uncle Ted found themselves out of work in 1911, and as their baby daughter had died they decided, with hundreds of others who, like themselves, had no prospect of better things at home, to emigrate to America or Canada. It was a hard and difficult decision. It meant leaving the old folks to fend for themselves, and leaving many friends and relations, but nevertheless, they felt urged to go.

Old Grandma, though heartbroken, had miraculously saved a few shillings in a tea-pot and said that they would have 'a reight good farewell do'. So they invited the aunts and uncles, sisters and brothers and others from far and wide. The people from whom they had borrowed chairs, knives, forks, spoons and cups expected to come as well, to reclaim their own. There was such a crush as never was as people came in through the front door as others were pushed out at the back, all in that little house, two up and two down, with flag floors and white-washed walls, a straw mattress on the bed and grandma's old wool stockings (when she could wear them no more) pulled up the table legs to stop them from being kicked and damaged with clogs.

'Quiet, everybody', said Grandad, who had been helped to his feet, 'on this solemn occasion when our Ted and Grace are about to leave their humble home to seek their fortune in a foreign land, we are gathered together to hope and pray that they will be prosperous and happy'. (Hear, hear). Somebody started to sing 'God be with you till we meet again', and with cries of 'We'll never see them again', they began to take back all the things they had lent. With much weeping and sobbing they left the family to themselves.

The emigrants were up early the next morning, and off to Liverpool. It was fifty years later when the only survivor from that 'farewell do' saw them again – they were not very prosperous, but they seemed to have been happy together.

Acknowledgements

I would like to thank all of the many people who have helped in the preparation and research for this book.

In particular, thanks go to all members of my family who have lived with this project for so long and who have encouraged me in its pursuit.

Thanks also to Dr Alan Crosby, who helped with the text and with the research for the many excellent illustrations.

Finally, thanks to Blackburn District Central Library, from whose excellent collection the photographs came, and who kindly allowed us to reproduce this selection.

The publishers would like to thank Lancashire County Libraries for their permission to reproduce the photographs in this book.